HOLY MAN SECULAR JOB

Encouragement for Those Called to Non-Clergy Careers

TOM MAY

First printing, July, 2009
© 2009 Tom May

Printed in the United States. All rights reserved.

ISBN: 978-0-9795394-9-7

All scripture quotations, unless otherwise indicated, are taken from the HOLY BIBLE, NEW INTERNATIONAL VERSION®. NIV®. Copyright © 1973, 1978, 1984 by International Bible Society. Used by permission of Zondervan. All rights reserved.

The author, Tom May can be contacted at tommayjr@verizon.net or through www.fatherspress.com

Father's Press

Lee's Summit, MO
(816) 600-6288
www.fatherspress.com
E-Mail: fatherspress@yahoo.com

Acknowledgements

To my wife, Teresa, who did the final editing and has obeyed the Lord's commandment to spur me on toward love and good works; especially finishing this book. May your book to pastor's wives be a strength, encouragement and comfort to many. Love always.

Special thanks to Alice Gray who graciously embraced the project of editing this book. I could not have done it without you. There has got to be a special crown for anyone who would edit an author's first book. Well done.

To my mentor, father and friend in the ministry, Pastor L. J. Johns. Because of your ministry to me I am able to minister to others. This book is part of your fruit.

To my Dad, Thomas May Sr., for teaching me, by example, the virtue of working to care for my family.

To God, my Savior, who is the Lord of the harvest. I pray for you to continue to send workers into every field and may they be encouraged through this book.

This book is dedicated to all of my Christian brothers and sisters who desire to make God known on their jobs by words and deeds. May you be known by your love for God and your love for one another.

Table of Content

Preface

Chapter One: Job Calling -------------- 1

Chapter Two: Prayer ------------------ 7

Chapter Three: Brotherhood ---------- 13

Chapter Four: Bible Study ------------ 21

Chapter Five: Integrity --------------- 35

Chapter Six: Evangelism -------------- 43

Chapter Seven: Persecution ----------- 49

Chapter Eight: Supervisors ----------- 63

Chapter Nine: Wages ----------------- 73

Chapter Ten: Controversy ------------ 79

Chapter Eleven: God's Final Exam---- 91

Preface

Have you ever wondered if the Lord really cares about where you work? Does He place value on your career? Does it make any difference to Him if you are a plumber or a pilot? Does He love pastors, evangelists and missionaries more than others? Does God view your job as being something more than just the source of a paycheck? Is being here on this job part of God's intentional plan or is it just filler in between becoming an adult and going to Heaven?

Most committed Christians have a desire to live their lives in a manner that would ignite a desire in their co-workers to follow Christ. However, their examples tend to be either the "soap box lunchroom preacher" or the "silent witness." Most of these Christians do not identify with either extreme. They are longing for practical ways to take what they are experiencing in their hearts and display it to those on their jobs.

In this book, I address these questions as well as many of the issues that most Christians grapple with throughout their careers. I believe that where we work and how we view our jobs has the possibility of having eternal significance. Therefore, God is very interested in our career and where we work. Our occupation is not just an afterthought in the mind of God.

I have written this book to give practical suggestions on how to be an effective witness for Christ on our jobs. It is about bringing glory to God by Him increasing and us decreasing. It is not a *how to* on getting a desired raise or promotion. It is not intended to instruct on how to make your day smooth and without problems. I have not written this book to show you how to get your unbelieving co-workers to be nice to you. It is not a book to teach you how to get the unbelieving to act like they are in church. It is about discovering ways to let the light that is within you shine so that men will glorify God and come to know Him.

I wrote this book from the viewpoint of a pastor who is working on a secular job. During the past 30 years of my career, I have worked in different environments and at different companies. I have worked for a small company with about ten employees, and I have worked at huge Fortune 500 companies. I have worked for both city and state governments. I have worked both full-time and part-time for churches where I was either the pastor or an assistant pastor. At various times, my sole source of income has come from working at a church, and at other times my income has come from working for a secular company.

Because of these job experiences, I believe that I am in a unique position to address many of the work-related issues of those who receive their income from sources that are other than the ministry. I believe very strongly that God wants to speak through a pastor who is working on a secular job. I thank Him for still using imperfect human beings such as myself. I also believe that His book is for pastors who seek to minister to God's flock. May God bless you in the reading of this book.

* By "the ministry" I am referring to church and parachurch organizations.

Presentation

This book is presented to

Receiver's Name

As a gift with best wishes for success by

Giver's Name   *Date*

Chapter 1

JOB CALLING

I am convinced that most Christians in the United States are not happy with their present job. They might not dislike their job, but they would rather be doing "something else." When asked what that something else is the majority would probably say, "I don't know." It has also been my observation that among truly committed Christians the something else is mostly some abstract vision of a full or part-time ministry.

Because of this mindset many Christians have adopted the belief that God does not care about what they do for a living, as long as it is honest. I believe that there are few things that are further from the truth. God immensely cares about every area of our lives, including our occupation. God has a "job calling" for each of us.

God's Calling for Our Livelihood

I firmly believe in God's calling or what may be termed as "His pre-ordained choice" for us in regards to what we do for a living. I believe He has ordained that Christians infiltrate every occupation under Heaven to be a witness to others in that same field. Of course, I am not referring to occupations that are definitely contrary to the Word of God. Paul made this clear when he wrote, "Nevertheless, each one should retain the place in life that the Lord assigned to him and to which God has called him. This is the rule I lay down in all the churches" (I Corinthians 7:17). Paul made this statement because he did not want the zealous new believers to think that they needed to quit their livelihood and leave their families to become missionaries all over the world. Paul recognized that his calling was different than others, and he did not want his readers to be confused about their calling. Heaven only knows how many times well-meaning, but misguided, Christians have sold all they had and went into the foreign mission field, but after arriving in a foreign country failed as missionaries. They might have listened to the missionary's call, but they had not received God's call. Because they failed, many were left with a shipwrecked faith. Having a heart for foreign missions does not necessarily mean that God wants you to go. It might just mean that he wants you to support those who have the calling.

The error on missing God's will for our occupation is not limited to the "secular" verses the "sacred." This is also true for our choice of one secular career over another. How many people have gone into careers because a well-meaning person or persons pushed them towards it? The person's God-given talents might have been in a totally different area. Along these lines, parents need to be on guard against the temptation of promoting their own vision for their child's life above God's vision for that child's life. "Train a child in the way *he* should go, and when he is old he will not turn from it" (Proverbs 22:6).

In order to abide in our calling, we must first seek God as to what He desires for our lives. There are some who have known all their lives, while others have taken the trial and error route. Many have multiple callings on their lives. It is possible that God will call you to one occupation earlier in life and then call you to another later in life. A typical example of multiple callings is a mother who had God's calling on her life to stay at home to raise her children. Once these children are grown and have left the nest God might place a calling on her life to enter a particular secular field or become more involved in church work. He might even call her to adopt a child to raise for the glory of God. I am sure that there are many Christian women who are in secular jobs because they automatically assumed that when their children were grown it was time for them to enter the workforce. We need to always seek God's face for every decision in our lives. When we pray to God, He will reveal to us what His will is in terms of our occupation.

The Benefits of Knowing Our Job Calling

There are at least five benefits to knowing what our job calling is and operating in it.

(1) When we operate in God's job calling, we tend to experience His divine approval. This is something that is intangible and subjective, but it is, nonetheless, real. We will not always feel God's approval any more than we will always feel saved, but there is a certain knowing that comes with the assurance that we are in the center of His will. The feeling is similar to what we feel when we are truly worshipping God. When we are truly worshipping God in spirit and truth, we are doing what we were created to do. In the same way, when we know and operate in our job calling, we have a certain knowing deep down in our spirit because we are doing what God created us for. We feel His approval.

(2) When we are operating in our job calling, we feel more secure about our own God given gifts. After all, we can't feel secure if we are uncertain about what are purpose in life is. When we are secure, we stop looking at what God has others to do and concentrate on what He has for our lives. We tend not to look at others and think: "I wish that were me up there singing." "I wish I could write books like him." "I wish I could teach the Word of God like that person." It is natural to admire the talents that God gives others, but it is not God's plan for your life to wish you had the gifts of others. God created us with our own job calling for His glory. Please do not rob Him of His glory by trying to be someone else. Know and operate in your own calling, and there will be security in your soul and peace in your heart.

(3) Knowing and operating in our job calling brings contentment and satisfaction, allowing us to focus on doing our job efficiently and accomplishing goals. When we accomplish our goals, we are content and satisfied with ourselves. Doing a better job and accomplishing goals also bring job promotions, which bring larger salaries.

(4) Knowing and operating in our job calling, we have a better attitude about our job and life. We are not upset so easily by work related problems. The mountains on the job do not seem so high and the valleys do not seem so low. When we are outside of our job calling, mole hills seem like mountains and pot holes seem like craters. If we enjoy what we believe God has called us to do, the time seems to fly by. If we do not enjoy it, the day seems to drag on.

(5) Knowing and operating in our divine job calling tends to cause us to be more pleasurable to be around. There are few things worse than having to work with people who hate their job. They are miserable and their attitude affects the work environment in a negative way. This point is important with regard to sharing our faith. If we are perceived as a grouch, we turn off our coworkers before we can even mention Jesus. Besides, they will think, "If Jesus is all that you say He is, how come you're so miserable?" Knowing and operating in God's job calling is important to every believer, and I hope we all come to believe that it is important to our heavenly Father, who created us for His glory. His glory shines through us when we are in the center of His will, therefore let us be in that position to let His light shine.

God has ordained for those in his church to be in different fields so that we can reach the lost that are in those particular fields. We live in such a very complex and hurried society that our lives are overflowing with everything that needs to be done. If we do not reach the lost while we are on our jobs, when and where will they be reached?

There are 168 hours in a week. This is my summation of the average week, broken down into hours.

56 hrs - sleep

40 hrs - work

10 hrs - travel to work

16 hrs - eating and food preparation

7 hrs - dressing and personal hygiene

4 hrs - church

17 hrs - household chores

6 hrs - help children with homework

3 hrs - finding things we lost

2 hrs - remembering the things we forgot

5 hrs - prayer and Bible reading

2 hrs - yelling at the kids

    Now I ask you again, when and where will we reach the lost if we do not reach them on our jobs? In addition, if we are not in jobs where we work with and next to non-believers, how will they ever hear the truth? How will they ever read the truth in our lives if we are not in a place where they spend time with us? The only things most non-believers know about church is what they hear about on the news. This information is almost always negative. With the network news as our public relations agency, we are not likely to have non-believers waiting in line to enter our churches to hear the gospel. We are in a public relations war with the media and the media is winning. The only way we can win is to take the offense by making one-on-one contacts to communicate with them by word and deed. Our goal is to communicate that there is a risen Savior. However, this cannot be accomplished unless we co-inhabit the areas where the lost are, which is primarily the workplace.

I believe that God has ordained teachers to reach teachers, janitors to reach janitors, factory workers to reach factory workers, lawyers to reach lawyers, politicians to reach politicians, managers to reach managers, musicians to reach musicians, and government workers to reach government workers.

This brings me to another point. We need more Christians in governmental positions. I believe there are present-day Daniels who God has called to become public officials that will be totally uncompromising and unwavering in their stand for righteousness. These are individuals who will not be swayed to form public policy based on opinion polls. They are those who are called to be true leaders, who would say to the public, "This is my stand on this issue and I hold it because it is the right position before God."

They are individuals who call sin what it is. They will stand for what is right, regardless of what it costs them. They will not turn their backs during the fight against abortion simply because it might cost them an election. They will stand because they are convinced in their hearts that the murder of innocent babies is an abomination and needs to be stopped. In the Book of Esther, Mordecai tells Esther in Chapter 4, Verse 14, "And who knows but that you have come to royal position for such a time as this?" The royal position was queen. Esther had been pre-ordained by God to be in this particular position of influence to halt the destruction of millions of Jewish lives.

It is possible that millions of Jewish and Slavic lives might have been spared in Nazi Germany if certain Christians had accepted their God-given calling to serve in the German government? They might not have been in a position to stop the murders, but they might have been in a position to reach others for Christ who would eventually be in a policy-making position. God has called Christians to various occupations of life to make a difference in the lives of people. Know what your calling is and "get at it."

Chapter 2

Prayer

If we are going to be effective in our daily Christian witness, especially on our jobs, we must be devoted to seeking the Lord in prayer. This cannot be thought of as optional. There is no substitute for prayer. It cannot be an after thought. Prayer cannot be viewed as a last resort. It is essential for everything that God has called us to do. Without it we are destined to failure. We are doomed to the futility and frustration of trying to accomplish the works of God by human means. There are many good ideas, but good ideas are not enough for such an important mission as reaching lost souls for the Lord. We need God's plan, and we only get that by spending time with Him in prayer.

Prayer Shows Concern for Others

I have made it a practice to pray for everyone that I work with by name before I go to work in the mornings. I pray for those who are Christians and those who are not Christians. I pray for their health, the health of their children, and any issues in their lives I am aware of. It is amazing how much people will open up to you when they find out that you are praying for their children. I ask them when I see them in the morning how their sick child is doing. They are touched by just the thoughtfulness of someone asking. How much more will they open up when they find out that you took the time to pray for their loved one? If unbelievers feel that you are concerned about the things that concern them, you have a greater chance of sharing the things that are most important to you, such as Jesus. For this reason, prayer is a very valuable tool of evangelism.

I am not talking about being phony. I am talking about a genuine heartfelt interest. The world can see through shallowness. One thing that I notice about Jesus is that He has a deep concern about people who are hurting. If you do not have an honest concern for people, you need to pray to the Lord to grant it to you. I believe that God will grant you your request. God is still looking for someone to stand in the gap so that judgment will not have to come upon man. Who knows if you are the only one standing in the way of God's judgment upon a co-worker or even a whole company? We have been called a kingdom of priest (1 Peter 2:9). The priests were the ones who would intercede for the people. I believe that we have been called to intercede for those who are on our jobs. Are we being the priests that God has called us to be? Are we crying out for their souls?

I do not know of anyone who has done a great work for God who was not devoted to prayer. The apostles realized how important prayer was to Jesus and asked Him to teach them how to pray. "One day Jesus was praying in a certain place. When He finished, one of His disciples said to Him, Lord, teach us to pray, just as John taught his disciples" (Luke 11:1). When the apostles asked Jesus why they were not able to cast a demon out of a boy, Jesus brought up the subject of prayer (Luke 9:29). Jesus prayed at Gethsemane before He was arrested. He even prayed while He hung on the cross. He said, "Father, forgive them, for they do not know what they are doing" (Luke 23:34). In Acts Chapter 2, the disciples were in prayer as they were earnestly expecting the promise of God. Nehemiah prayed and he found favor with the king of Persia (Nehemiah 2:11). Daniel prayed and received revelation (Daniel 9:3-4).

In sharing my views on prayer, I do not mean to imply that I consider myself to be a great prayer warrior. Sometimes I struggle to get out of bed in the mornings to pray. There are times when I lack the excitement to pray. In fact, I must confess, sometimes prayer for me is a chore. Sometimes it flows and sometimes it does not. There are mornings when I have an intimate time with the Lord, and other mornings when He has had to put notes in my lunch bag. Some mornings I leave the throne room of God overflowing with his Spirit and so excited that I am ready to take on the devil with one hand tied behind my back. At other times, I feel like my prayers never got above the ceiling. I know what Jesus meant when He said, "Watch and pray, that ye enter not into temptation: the spirit indeed is willing, but the flesh is weak" (Matthew 26:41 KJV).

I do not want to attempt to dictate the length of time we pray, but I believe that there is great merit in seeking the Lord at the start of each day. It makes perfect sense to me to get my instructions for the day before I start the work. It is wise to check in with the architect before you build your house. Police officers attend a briefing before they start their shift. Pilots attend a briefing before they fly their airplanes. Soldiers get instructions from their commanding officers before they leave their base to face the difficult situations of battle. If getting instruction for starting a task is so vital for those who perform earthly services, how much more is it essential for those who perform heavenly service? We need to meet with our commanding office, the Lord Jesus Christ, before we start our mission for that day. How long the meeting lasts might vary, but the important thing is that by the time we start the mission, we have touched the heart of God and He has touched our hearts.

Praying Appropriately for the Situation

Paul says in 1 Thessalonians 5:17, "Pray without ceasing." By this I believe God desires us to always be in constant communication with Him. We should always have our spiritual "walkie-talkies" on so that we can be in constant communication with Him in every situation. For this reason I do not agree with those who teach that prayer has to be always audible. There are some circumstances on the job when an audible prayer is not advisable, but communication with God is. You might have to be in a one-on-one meeting with a supervisor who is criticizing some aspect of your job performance. This is probably not the best time for you to blurt out an audible prayer. Wisdom dictates that prayer is in order, but silent prayer is preferred as well as more effective. If we deny ourselves of silent prayer, we rob ourselves of precious communion with God during many critical times. Both audible and silent prayers are important, but it is also important to know when to use each.

Prayer is an appropriate combat weapon in spiritual warfare. The Bible teaches that the ruler of this world has blinded the eyes of unbelievers so that they cannot see the truth (2 Corinthians 4:4). This biblical truth became very clear to me one day when I shared the gospel with a man whom I worked with. I knew that I had done a good job in sharing the gospel. I had plenty of time to do so, and I gave the Word of God with good illustrations, but I just was not getting through to him. I could tell that he heard what I was saying, but he still had no understanding of what I was expressing to him. God revealed to me that Satan was keeping him from understanding what I was saying. This was an instance that the only affective weapon I had was prayer. In such circumstances as this one, we must pray for God to take the demonic veil from over the person's mind so that person can understand. Once that veil is removed, that person can clearly see the fork in the road and decide which route to take.

True evangelism is getting people to the point of making a decision. The devil has blinded the minds of most unbelievers to the point that they do not even know that there is a decision to be made. When we prevail in prayer for unbelievers, we bring them to that place where they are forced to make a decision. They are forced to choose whom they will serve. At this point we must be ready to pray with some to receive Jesus as their Lord and Savior. We must also be ready to endure the wrath of those who choose to reject the Lord.

Intercessory prayer, or praying for others, is also a powerful spiritual weapon. James 5:16 say, ". . . pray for each other so that you may be healed. The prayer of a righteous man is powerful and effective." I pray for the other Christians on my job. I pray for their encouragement, protection, spiritual maturity, and witnessing opportunities. If they are sick, I pray for them to be healed. Intercessory prayer is one way of carrying one another's load. I know that God is pleased when we show our concern for our

Christian brothers and sisters by lifting them up in prayer. I believe He loves to answer intercessory prayers that benefit His children.

Praying for One Another

I want to add here that we need to make our needs known to the other saints so they can be blessed by praying for us. Praying for one another is a way to build unity, trust, and dependency. I depend upon the prayers of my Christian co-workers. The prayer request does not have to be overly personal. It can be as general as asking your Christian co-worker to pray for you to complete a project on time or do well on a presentation. However, this prayer of agreement draws your brother or sister closer to you and unites the two of you in a common goal. There are many close allies who would be enemies if they were not working for a common goal. Goals bind people together who otherwise would have no association at all. On any great team, there are individuals who have major differences, but all the great teams are able to put away their differences to achieve a common goal.

Paul says in 1Timothy 2:2 to pray for all who are in authority. Those in authority include our bosses. Praying for them keeps our hearts right before God as well as our supervisor. Paul says we need to pray for those in authority so that we can live peaceful and quiet lives. In 1Timothy 2:4, he says that God wants "all men to be saved." There is a definite relationship between our supervisors being saved and us having a quiet and peaceful life on our jobs. If our supervisors are walking according to the Word of God, we are in a better position to prosper. Since prosperity and conflict do not generally go together, we need to pray for the salvation of our supervisors so that we may live in peace and prosper.

There are many thoughts in this book on how to be an effective witness for Christ on our jobs. However, I am convinced that none of them will have long term success if prayer is not a major part of what we do. Commit to the LORD whatever you do, and your plans will succeed (Proverbs 16:3).

Chapter 3

Brotherhood

Over the years of working on secular jobs, I have observed that Christians fellowship more with non-believers than with other Christians. This situation bothers me because 1 Peter 2:17 tells us to love the brotherhood. In other words, Christians ought to love the fellowship of one another. When we value the company of non-believers more than that of believers, we tell the world that we do not want to be around other Christians. We tell non-believers we want to be like them.

Why would non-believers want to become Christians if the Christians they know are seeking to become like them? Are we showing non-believers by our association with them that there is greater value in being with them than with the Church? Are non-believers thinking, "Why should I come to a fellowship at a church if the church members do not want to be around their own members?" The even greater question might be, "Are we telling Jesus that fellowship outside His body is preferable to inside His body?"

At this point, some of you may be saying, "He is telling me to stay away from non-believers." No, I am not. I am not advocating extreme isolationism in which Christians do not have any contact with non-believers. This idea is not biblical. When Jesus prayed for the church in Chapter 17 of the Gospel of John, He did not asked the Father to take it out of the world, but to keep it while it was in the world. However, in the same prayer, Jesus asked the Father to make us one as He and the Father are one. Therefore, we cannot be one if we do not fellowship with one another. A Christian whose inner most friends and associates are all non-believers, either on the job or off, is a shame and a reproach to the name of Christ. Jesus associated with others, but all of His close friends were His disciples and followers.

There have been non-believers on and off my job who I enjoyed being with because we shared the same interest and they were pleasant to be with. But when it comes to a choice between them and the family of God, the family is where my allegiance lies. II Corinthians 6:14 says, "Do not be yoked together with unbelievers." I am sure that the Godhead is grieved when His children prefer the comradeship with unbelievers over fellowshipping with others in the family.

Of course, I am not so naive as to believe that we will always enjoy every Christian's company 24 hours a day. There is always friction when the ways and views of others are totally different and sometimes opposing to ours. But love covers a multitude of sins (1 Peter 4:8) as well as differences. Remember God demonstrated His love toward us when we were sinners and unlovely by sending Jesus Christ to die for us. Furthermore, He shows His love to us now by giving us grace and mercy in spite of our many faults and failures. If the God in us is as big as we claim, we can forebear with patience others who Christ has redeemed and are still on the journey towards spiritual maturity. I would imagine that the temptation was ever before Jesus to say to Peter, "Why don't you think before you open your mouth?" or to say to him, "You're full of hot air!" But the Lord looked beyond Peter's faults and saw what he could become and said to him, "Simon, Simon, Satan has asked to sift you as wheat, but I have prayed for you, Simon, that your faith may not fail. And when you have returned to Me, strengthen your brothers" (Luke 22:31-32). Jesus' comment to Peter also applies to us. We ought to be strengthening our brothers and sisters. We ought to be kindly affectionate to one another (Romans 12:10) and share one another's burdens (Galatians 6:2). Now if we do not fellowship with one another, how are we going to carry out these two responsibilities to one another?

One of the reasons I believe Christians do not fellowship with other Christians on their jobs is the mis-interpretation of Hebrews 10:25. This scripture says, "Let us not give up meeting together, as some are in the habit of doing, but let us encourage one another and all the more as you see the day approaching." There are too many that see this scripture as meaning exclusively that Christians need to go to church. I believe that this scripture was meant to be broader in its application. I believe Paul is saying in this scripture that when saints come together for strength, encouragement, and exhortations, we need to be with them.

I have heard Christians say, "I go to church on Sundays and I attend a midweek service. I don't need to attend a Bible study at work." I cannot stress how wrong this attitude is. The underlying thinking behind this attitude is that the only time we need other Christians is on Sunday mornings and Wednesday nights and we do not need them while we are on the job or elsewhere. When we think this way we do not properly comprehend the purpose of Christ's Body. You cannot say that the only time we need encouragement and edification is on Sundays and Wednesday nights. We cannot say that the only time we need to spur one another on towards love and good deeds is on Sunday and Wednesday nights.

The Body of Christ is a gift to each individual part for the purpose of aiding that part by way of nourishment, protection, comfort, healing, and care. God's gifts do not stop once the church building's lights are off and the doors are closed behind us. We cannot restrict the functioning of the Body of Christ to a building or a particular time once or twice a week. Jesus said, "For where two or three come together in My name, there am I with them" (Matt.18:20). Whenever two or more believers get together, there is a concentration of God's gifts and power.

A prideful Christian says, "Gathering together is all right for those who are weak, but I can stand on my own." Every Christian needs every bit of Christian fellowship he or she can get. If you are fortunate enough to have other Christians at your workplace, you need to have fellowship with them as well as pray with them. You need them! They need you! We all need each other! It is sheer folly for there to be a Bible study or a Christian sharing group at your job and you never participate in it.

The individuals in the Bible study or Christian sharing group might not believe everything exactly the way you believe, do everything exactly the way you do it, or say everything the way you say it, but barring the teaching of "another gospel" (Galatians 1:6-7) in the group meeting, we need to avail ourselves of the spiritual gifts that are resident in each Christian. Since God has placed different gifts in each of us that can help or encourage the Body of Christ as a whole, we must fellowship with one another to obtain the help and encouragement we need in our lives. On my jobs, I have seen God make personnel changes to make sure His children have the fruits of fellowship. I have seen him pair-up Christians in a department to strength each other in their Christian walk and encourage each other in their work.

Furthermore, without good wholesome fellowship with each other, there is no tangible display of love for non-believers to see. I remember hearing the story of two first cousins who were in the same class in high school. They even had the same last name and grew up right around the corner from each other. However, no one had any idea that they were related. This is the view that non-believers have of professing Christians. Since they do not see us together, they do not see us as relatives. Without good wholesome fellowship with each other, there is no tangible display of love among us for non-believers to see. Jesus said, "By this all men will know that you are My disciples, if you love one another" (John 13:35).

The doctrine of separation of churches and denomination is also a reason why many Christians do not want to fellowship with other Christians on the job. I am sorry to say that this doctrine is the result of Sunday sermons that focus on disharmony and distrust of Christians that do not believe as that particular church does. Much of this teaching is based on hear say stories about other churches or denominations. Many of these stories resemble stories of man-eating cannibals in lands that we never heard of. No one has ever seen them, but they must exist because someone heard someone else say that their fourth cousin said that they overheard that some person said that they were told about these ferocious man-eating something or others in some far off land.

I have had the advantage of visiting many of the major denominations and Christian movements of our time in my travels. I would say that about 90 percent of the weird stuff that you hear about them are either not true, misinterpreted, or ultra extremes which do not represent the thoughts of the majority. Quite often many preachers get stories from individuals who do not clearly know what another organization teaches or has taught. Too often, these preachers do not check these stories out for themselves. They just repeat the hearsay because it supports their position. My prayer is that we become seekers of truth and avoid hearsay.

Another hindrance to Christian fellowship may be language differences. We do not all use the same dictionary of Christian terms. What one group means by one term, another group might mean something different. There are groups that have their own vocabulary. You can recognize them by their "buzz words." Some groups are so concerned about being absolutely correct with every word that they put themselves in bondage and try to lock the prison door on everyone else, too. They do this at the expense of true brotherhood and love. These groups tend to not mix well with other saints. We might be correct in our terminology, but we must always remember to act in love. And so what if someone has a few theological terms mixed up? Are they still our brothers and sisters? I do not say to a five year old, "No stupid, this word only means one thing and I won't play with you until you get it straight." There have been senseless squabbling over terms of salvation such as saved, redeemed, born-again, Christian, born-again Christian, saint, and believer in Christ. All of these terms are synonymous. We must be careful not to allow a fear of certain terms that are foreign to us, to build walls of distrust between us.

Another barrier to Christian fellowship at the workplace is culture, background, and things that we have assumed without really thinking about them. We have devolved to the days of the Book of Judges where every man's ways are right in his own eyes

(Judges 21:25). We tend to believe that "It's my way or the wrong way."

I was rummaging through a box one day and happened to run across a crucifix that was given to me when I was at a retreat a few years earlier. It was a rather grotesque looking figure. As I picked it up and looked at it, the thought came to me that I had been slack regarding my witnessing. Then I thought that by wearing it around my neck it would serve as a conversation piece. The people at my job knew that I was not a Catholic so they would ask me why I was wearing it. It is great when you do not have to initiate the conversation. They cannot accuse you of preaching then because you are merely answering their questions. I was "called to the carpet" by fellow Christians. I have heard things such as, "You shouldn't wear that crucifix because Jesus isn't on the cross anymore." I am sorry to say, that because of their perspective, they missed the whole point. There are many fine Christians who wear crucifixes as a reminder to themselves of what Jesus went through for them. Once again, it is more a matter of perspective and culture than it is of right or wrong. We must be so careful not to judge and condemn when we do not have all the facts. One of the first things that we must do to correct this attitude is to realize that there are valid ways of doing things that might not have originated at our church or in our denomination. We must allow God to do something different at the church across the street as well as in another Christian's life.

The final area which keeps Christians from fellowshipping together on their jobs is "spiritual pride." It is the "I've got something you don't have" spirit. This is the "my church is better than your church" attitude. This prideful spirit may be the most destructive tool that the devil has. It is great to be proud of our church and to speak highly of it, but it is not right for us to say or imply that our church is "Spiritual Jerusalem." I have had someone tell me that I was still of the world because I did not attend his church. Spiritual arrogance only fosters resentment. Likewise, we get the same reaction from non-believers when we come to them with a prideful attitude. Jesus did not flaunt His superior knowledge or power to His disciples or anyone else.

Now I realize that there are good and bad churches. There are churches that teach the Bible and there are those that do not, but people will never leave their bad churches and come to your good church if you do not show them by your godly lifestyle and attitude that your church is changing your life for the better. If we attack a person's tradition, church, club or denomination, they will defend their group, even if that group has all the problems that you say. People do not like to be told that they made a wrong decision, and they will either attack you or shut you completely out. At this point we have no communication, no fellowship, no love and therefore no witness.

Let us stop using the Word of God as a bat to attack others with. If we do use it as such, those that we hit with it will either fight back or run away from us. Each bat has a label on it. But I can guarantee you that no one is going to try to read that label when the bat is being swung at them. It also does not help if while we are swinging that bat to say, "You just don't believe the Bible." or "You are just being rebellious and stubborn against God." The person that says, "I am going to get him to see this scripture my way if it kills him!" is operating in spiritual pride and not love. I have heard preachers berate other Christians because they could not get them to accept their interpretation of a particular scripture. They resort to belittling, slander, and name calling. When they do these things, they are operating in spiritual arrogance and not the love of God. If the truth were really known, most of the time the reason behind our vehement emotions lies within our ungodly pride because we personally cannot stand for someone to disagree with us. It becomes a personal matter that we dress up in spiritual garb and try to use God against someone who holds a different opinion.

I am a person who tends to be very uncompromising in my convictions, but I realize that anything said or done that does not have love at its core is just noise. Paul expressed this in I

Corinthians 13:1: "If I speak in the tongues of men and of angels, but have not love, I am only a resounding gong or a clanging cymbal." When we share our convictions, the finished product ought to produce faith, hope, and love. And the greatest of these is love (1 Corinthians 13:38).

Chapter 4

Bible Studies

I think it should be quite clear by now that I believe that consistent fellowship with the saints is important. Because I am so committed to this idea, I have pushed for and supported over the years Bible studies on the job. I have learned through experience they are far more than just gatherings to study the Bible. They are hospitals where people are healed of both physical and emotional pains. They are arenas for learning and expanding ideas. They are counseling sessions where Christians can bring their problems. They are forums in which concerns are raised. They are foreign ports where spiritual supplies are obtained. They are electrical outlets where spiritual batteries are recharged. They are times of sharing victories and defeats. They are times to meet needs and have needs met. They are oases in the middle of a rough workday. They are good places where future mates are met and the launch pad of lifelong friendships. They are places to hear a different perspective. They are great sites for evangelism because you can sometimes get non-believers to attend them who you would not be able to persuade to attend a church service. Bible studies tend to be seen as more of a neutral place rather than a church.

The workplace Bible studies I have been associated with have been during lunch break. I know of other successful ones that have been before working hours. The time depends on what is best for the group.

Drafted to Start a Bible Study

When there was not a Bible study on two of my jobs, I started one. Both of them were at large companies. I had little choice in starting the first one. At that time I worked for a company that not only occupied several buildings in a large business complex but also had buildings in other locations. When I joined the company, there was already a Bible study club that included some 10-15

Bible studies which met in different buildings. The company allowed the club to use its conference rooms for Bible study as long as it did not interfere with company business.

I knew most of the professing Christians in my building that housed 200-300 employees. However, I noticed that most of them did not know any more than one or two of the others. Through prayer it came to me to have one big, one-time acquaintance meeting of all the Christians in the building. I was going to put up signs that said, "Christians come meet your family!" I had not told anyone about this idea at this point. Well, one week turned into two, and the two weeks turned into three. I admit I dragged my feet.

Then God took matters into His own hands. Unknown to me, a meeting had taken place between two women at the copying machine room. The first lady said to the second lady who was in charge of copies, "I attend a Bible study in another building, but it is so far away. By the time I get over there, it's time for me to come back. Wouldn't it be nice if we had one here in our building?" Just at that time another lady came up and heard the first two talking. The third lady said, "It would be wonderful to have a Bible study here." At just that time, a man came up and joined in the conversation. Outside of the first two, none knew the others were Christians. I knew all of them, but they did not know that each of them knew me. You can probably guess what happened after this. My name came up as the choice to lead this Bible study. I was not drafted to go to Vietnam, but God's selective service had my number. The group was in total agreement, so they picked up a fifth person and came after me. I was cornered by them in the hallway and informed of my rights. The only right I had was to decide which day the Bible study was going to be on. I felt like Jonah.

I cannot begin to tell you what a blessing the study was for all of us. At the first meeting, there was about eight of us. This number grew to the point where we had as many as 25 attending. In fact, during the six years that I lead the Bible study, the biggest problem we faced was to find rooms large enough for all of us to meet in. We must have outgrown two different conference rooms.

Those who attended were so excited about the Bible study that they began to tell Christians in other buildings about it. A number of them began to come to the Bible study. Some of them who only had 30 minutes for lunch were coming just to be able to spend as little as 15 minutes with their brothers and sisters. Now we faced a new dilemma. With the group being so large, not everyone was able to join in and share. This is one of the drawbacks when the group gets too large. Some of the saints who either did not know as much about the Bible or who just were not outspoken as others started to be left out of the sharing. It was not that the group was insensitive to their needs; it was just that quiet temperaments sometimes were lost in large crowds.

On top of this, for order sake, I was being pushed from a position of leader to being *the teacher*, a position I did not desire. I did not mind teaching the scriptures. I loved it. It is my calling. The problem was that the whole atmosphere of the study was changing. As just the leader, all I basically did was keep order, which I rarely even had to do, and either closed in prayer or asked someone else to close in prayer. In this position, I could be just "one of the boys." With me teaching the study, the group would be reduced to more of a formal teaching session with only a few ever being able to express themselves. I sought the Lord on this because I was feeling a burden. I found out later that others were also praying.

God soon solved our over-population problem. He placed in the hearts of the Christians from one of the other buildings to start their own study at their own workplace. Most of the time, when the word "split" is mentioned in a Christian setting, we think of something negative. However, this was the most natural and easy division I have ever experienced. There was no turmoil or jealousy and no hard feelings or resentment. There was just joy and deep down conviction that this was of the Lord. There was visiting back and forth to both Bible studies and no one was asked, "What are you doing over here or why are you going over there?" There was just love and peace. There was no competition.

The diversity within the group was a true witness to the others in the building. We had Baptist, Lutheran, Pentecostals, Presbyterians, members of the Church of Christ, Charismatics, Catholics, Brethrens, Independents, Episcopalians, and members of non-denomination churches. Denomination was never an issue. If you had asked any of us what we were, you would not have gotten "I'm a Baptist," "I'm a Catholic, or some other denomination. You simply would hear, "I'm a Christian." We were Black, White, and Hispanic, male and female. We were from all levels of education from Ph.D. to not even a high school diploma. We had varied backgrounds and cultures. There were department managers, secretaries, section heads, technicians and mail-room workers. Outsiders knew who was a part of the group, but they could not understand how there could be such love and unity with such diversity. From time to time, we would have non-believers visit us. A couple of those wanted what we had and they professed Christ. We had others who recommitted their lives to the Lord. We were all one in the Lord. In our own small way, we had achieved the unity of Christ without half trying, because we truly loved the Lord and each other and it was seen by all.

As a side note, those Christians who for whatever reason did not attend were not looked down upon, but were treated by all with love and respect. This is a very important point. I have talked very strongly about Christian fellowship on the job, but I do not ever want to imply that every Christian who does not attend a Bible study is in sin or rebellious. This attitude is destructive to the cause of Christ and unity within the body.

There were a few Christians who did not totally understand how God was pulling this miracle off. In the beginning, I was criticized by some well-meaning Christians for not dogmatically picking and choosing doctrines which others held which were incorrect and then attacking them. I never believed that God had called me to that group to be a false doctrinal "hit man." There are those who are in the body who look for fights. This was not our approach. We simply started in one book of the Bible and examined it verse by verse. We started off with First John. As we went through this epistle, some would share how a certain verse had particular significance to them or how their life was changed by obtaining understanding of that verse. Others would say that they never thought very much about a particular verse until someone else had shared his or her viewpoint. None of us were naive enough to think that everyone was going to agree on everything, but we did respect everyone's feelings and treated everyone as we expected everyone to treat us.

My conviction is that I cannot change anyone's opinion on a particular verse. That is the Holy Spirit's job. He has got to prove the scripture to that individual's heart. I can teach, talk, preach, scream, and explain my viewpoint fifty different ways, but unless a person is seeking the truth and the Holy Spirit convicts that individual of that truth, I am wasting both of our time. Sometimes all we can do is toss seeds and hope that one of the seeds takes root.

As we went through various controversial passages, I relied more on the Holy Spirit than my ability to blow someone else's precious "doctrinal rubber dingy" out of the water. When there were differences, we just merely expressed our opinions and kept moving. It was never long before we got to a passage that we all agreed upon and soon forgot what we had disagreed upon.

I feel that it is as important to know why people feel or believe the way they do as it is to know how and what they feel and believe. Feelings and beliefs tend to be symptoms of something deeper. To a certain extent, we are all products, for better or worse, of what we have been taught by others. We have been told things by people who we have looked up to all our lives or by an individual who led us to the Lord that were not totally correct. The problem with getting information is that you cannot always remember if you received it from your own studies or you just accepted it as truth from someone who you respect. This may be the biggest wall we must face when we try to understand another's viewpoint.

I remember one time when we were in the Gospel of Matthew; we came to the scripture in Chapter 12 where it mentioned Jesus' brothers. There were some Christians who religiously attended the study who happened to be lifelong Catholics. In fact one of them was a man who was born and raised in Mexico. Now this may not mean much to most, but if you know anything about Catholic doctrine and especially the emphasis in a Mexican Catholic church, these calm and peaceful waters had all the potential to become a 100-foot tidal wave. First of all for those who do not know Catholic doctrine, Mary is held in very high esteem. If you ever want to make a quick enemy, just imply that Mary was not a virgin before Jesus was born. However, this was not what the potential conflict was about. The Roman Catholics teach Mary never had sex before Jesus was born and she remained a virgin for the rest of her life. In other words, she never had any sexual relations with Joseph, even after Jesus was born. The idea that Mary gave birth to other children besides Jesus did not bother the rest of us one bit, but it caused our dear Catholic brother to become openly emotional. I had gone over the passage of scriptures to be discussed at the Bible study the day before and knew that it might be a source of controversy, but I was not prepared for his reaction. We discussed the issue for maybe 10-15 minutes, which was all the time we had left for the Bible study. Our Mexican brother was visibly shaking when we all left after the closing prayer.

Although we who were not Catholic did not agree with the Catholic doctrine, we treated our Catholic brothers and sisters with love and respect. None of us had hard feelings towards each other, including our Mexican brother because in his heart he knew we all deeply loved him and that he loved us. I went to see this brother later. He had calmed down and we greeted each other warmly. I reaffirmed my love for him and calmly shared with him from the scriptures why I believed Mary had other children. I knew he was a man who deeply loved the scriptures. He calmly said, "I understand why you believe the way you do." It had been difficult for him to understand at the Bible study when so many different people were talking, sometimes all at once.

I had not gone down to "convert" him. My motive was just to get him to understand why I believe what I do and to let him know that I understand why he believes the way he does. By the way, he never did say that he agreed with my view. But that is all right because it was now up to the Spirit of Truth to reveal the truth to both of our hearts. Our Catholic brothers and sisters never stopped attending the Bible study. I witnessed them growing along with the rest of us in knowledge and love for our Lord and Savior. Sure, there were other issues which came up as we went through the scripture, but we weathered all the storms as we fulfilled Christ's command. "Love one another."

A Bible Study Attacked

The second Bible study I started was at a site that was some distance from the central location of the large company. This meant that rather than thousands of people, we only had contact with about a hundred. The circumstances were different, but I felt ever so strongly that there needed to be one in my building. I had only been at the company for three weeks before we had our first Bible study. I had remembered the three-week episode with my first Bible study, and I was not about to let procrastination take hold of me again. The news of the formation of this study was spread by word of mouth. The Lord blessed me by making sure that my first close work-mate was a Christian. (I thank God for providing me with this daily Christian companionship!) He had worked for the company for a while and so he knew all the professing Christians. His knowing them saved me time in having to search for all of them on my own.

We started the Bible study with four people. I think that the most that we ever had was eight or nine. Once again we had Christians from varied backgrounds. Of the four of us, no one was from the same denomination, but we all loved the Lord. Within a couple of weeks we had six that represented six different denominations. I mentioned that the circumstances were different for this Bible study. We had opposition from the start. Though it had been tried here before, no past Bible study had lasted over a month. We had individuals in the building who were against it. We would hear statements like "You can't do that here. You're just asking for trouble."

The first Bible study I started took off like a rocket. This one was to be trench warfare. I believe as Ephesians Chapter 6 teaches that we are in a fight against evil spiritual forces. I do not believe that there is a demon under every rock or that whenever something bad happens, from a flat tire to a sniffle, that it is the devil attacking us. I do believe, however, that if you serve the Lord long enough you are bound to have some kind of confrontation with demonic activity in one form or another.

Within the first six months of the start of the Bible study, we experienced direct demonic attack. Two attendees began to have severe financial difficulties, one of which was fired for doing something that was totally out of his character. The other of the two had a wife who battled with unusual depression during this time. The wife of one brother had two miscarriages. This same brother was constantly missing work because of various illnesses. Another member of the group went into deep depression and was thoroughly convinced that she was going to be fired and then was convinced that she had an incurable disease and was going to die. She ended up having to spend time in a psychiatric ward. Another of the group had a glass beaker blow up in his face. I myself had colds or flu repeatedly for the entire six months. A few of us were plagued with car problems during this period.

Upon further investigation I discovered that before I came to the company, there had been another saint who had been very zealous in sharing the gospel of Jesus Christ. It seems that two tragic events happened in that saint's life shortly after she started witnessing for Jesus. These events were enough to totally sideline her and she was left spiritually bankrupt. At the point that I left the company, she was still in the state that I met her.

I was now convinced that we were up against evil spiritual forces that were going to fight us to defeat any move of God. I voiced my concerns to the other saints. I wish I could say that we were all in agreement, but we were not. There were some who because of their church's doctrinal position, believed that all demonic activity died out during the apostolic era, therefore, they believed that the events were all coincidental. I did not want to invoke a doctrinal squabble, so I just talked privately to those who believed as I did. I asked them to join me in daily praying for protection of each one of the saints in our building and our families. I also asked them to join me in praying to God against these evil forces.

I would like to be able to say that everything was smooth sailing after this, but it was not. However, most of the major problems ceased soon after we started to pray. The brother whose wife had the miscarriage soon conceived again and this time gave birth to a healthy boy. My health problems ceased. The automobile problems subsided. The study was doing well. I believe that prayer truly makes a difference. When we pray in unity and faith it makes a big difference. James says, "The effectual fervent prayers of a righteous man availeth much."(KJV)

As I mentioned before, not all were in agreement, but I think it is important to work with those we are able to work with. This does not mean that we separate ourselves from the others who did not see it our way. You might find that there will be some who you will be able to work with on one occasion, but will be in total disagreement with you the next time. The reverse also holds true.

There are three things that I did not do that maintained and even furthered our unity as a Bible study group. First, I did not attempt to impose my church's program or agenda on the rest of the group. Secondly, I totally resisted an *"us* versus *them* crusade." Thirdly, we treated the others as if there had been total agreement all along. One of the main purposes of a workplace Bible study is to promote unity among the body of Christ. Therefore, we ought to resist the things that would hinder this goal.

Another difference with respect to this Bible study was in regards to my role within the study. I have had to walk the fine line of, on the one hand, being *a* leader, and on the other hand, not being *the* leader. This challenge was tough at times. People tend to want to elevate those who they perceive are more spiritual or who know more about the Bible. Because of our particular work circumstances, this had trouble written all over it. First of all, we were a totally unofficial group which the upper management knew little or nothing about, which suited me just fine. To them we were just individuals who got together about once a week to exchange ideas, even though I am sure some were watching us very closely. In our position, it was unwise to have someone who appeared to be "calling the shots." Having someone being *the* leader becomes even more undesirable when the person leading is also a pastor of a church. The last thing I wanted to hear was, "He is trying to run a church on the job."

Those of you who are pastors who still work on a secular job need to pay careful attention to this point. You are not judged with the same rules as everyone else, either by your company's management, unbelievers or even by other Christians. The King James Version of the Bible say in I Thessalonians 5:22, "Abstain from all appearance of evil." The Bible also says that we need to be as wise as serpents (Matthew 10:16). I am not saying that you should not lead an unofficial Bible study, but you need to make sure you understand the risk of incurring the uncertain actions of both fellow employees and the management. All you would need is just one person to voice his displeasure or say you are trying to force him to believe as you. Management would probably shut the Bible study down and forbid you from meeting again or sharing your faith.

The first Bible study was officially recognized because there were many other officially recognized clubs on-site. There were no official clubs in the second. Because of the above, especially being a pastor, being *the* leader presented a very fine line to walk. This is why it was important for me to be one of the leaders and not *the* leader. This is not to say that you do not have or need leadership. I am saying that leadership does not necessarily mean "one man" rule.

Keys for a Bible Study Leader

I would like to share with you two keys in how to be a leader without being *the* leader. These are humility and the promotion of a plurality of leadership.

Humility- Humility and pride are at the opposite ends of the spectrum. They are like oil and water, they do not mix. They can not exist together. Pride is a perpetual condition of our sinful nature. Humility is an ongoing work of the Holy Spirit within us. In the book of Micah, the prophet writes, "He has showed you, O man, what is good. And what does the LORD require of you? To act justly and to love mercy and to walk humbly with your God." (Micah 6:8)

The Lord desires for all of us to walk humbly before Him, but this is particularly important for leadership. Humility in leadership sets the course for those who follow. We have the perfect example of this in Jesus. In His letter to the Philippians, Paul uses Jesus as an example of a leader who exemplifies humility. "Each of you should look not only to your own interests, but also to the interests of others. Your attitude should be the same as that of Christ Jesus: Who, being in very nature God, did not consider equality with God something to be grasped, but made Himself nothing, taking the very nature of a servant, being made in human likeness. And being found in appearance as a man, He humbled Himself and became obedient to death – even death on a cross! (Philippians 2:4-8)

Jesus spent very important time teaching His twelve apostles on the subject of humility.

Mathew 20:25 Jesus called them together and said, "You know that the rulers of the Gentiles lord it over them, and their high officials exercise authority over them.
26 Not so with you. Instead, whoever wants to become great among you must be your servant,
27 and whoever wants to be first must be your slave—
28 just as the Son of Man did not come to be served, but to serve, and to give His life as a ransom for many."

In this passage, Jesus admonishes the apostles to not be like the Gentiles in their form of leadership. I particularly want to focus on the phase, "lord it over them." Those who desire to be *the leader*, have a tendency to lord over people. They want to be in control. They do not feel comfortable with someone else being in charge. In the Philippians passage it says, "He humbled Himself," Pride will always drive us to be above others, but humility will prompt us to lower ourselves to lift others up. I was taught that true leadership in the Kingdom of God is to serve in such a way that you work yourself out of a job. We can only do this by lifting others up to serve just as well. In doing this we show godly leadership and bring glory to God, and not to ourselves.

If we prefer our fellow Christians above ourselves, we will not become a prideful leader. Jesus gave the apostles another lesson in godly leadership when He washed their feet. Here, the King of Glory led by putting others first. A person walking in pride would never dream of doing this and it is the same pride that would lead to the demise of the Bible study. "Pride goes before destruction, a haughty spirit before a fall." (Proverbs 16:18)

I believe that if we humble ourselves, God will bring the proper promotion within the group. I have seen God raise and lower my level of participation as He felt it was needed. There are times when I hardly said anything the whole time we were together. So often we can stifle emerging leadership as well as heartfelt vocalized needs if we are too dominant. God has a way of balancing everything out, but we make things flow so much better when we are humble.

Plurality of Leadership. I have tried to promote the idea of the "plurality of leadership." When I use this term, I mean that there is more than one person who is able to lead and make decisions in the group. The last thing I want is for the group not to meet if one person, *"The Leader,"* is not available at the time of the study or leaves the company.

Plurality of leadership adds a great deal more stability to Bible studies than single leadership. Bible studies, as well as churches, whose foundation is a single stone fall quickly when that stone is removed. We all want to be a part of something that will last. By promoting a plurality of leadership, we increase the chances of long-lasting success. Many of us have heard of churches that appeared strong crumbling soon after a popular pastor left. These churches were built on a single personality. Promoting plurality of leadership also assures that the Bible study does not slump or not meet at all if one or two key people are not there. The old saying "one monkey don't stop no show" is true as long as you have others who are already operating in leadership. We need to promote personal growth, not dependency.

If you are one leader among many, strategically, you are better protected in the case of persecution from the management. It is always easier to hit a big stationary target. If for some reason, contention arises because of the gospel, it is much easier to point to one single leader as the problem. It is not likely that a company would take disciplinary action against a whole group. Plurality of leadership provides protection because there is safety in numbers.

Another advantage of plurality of leadership is that you are better able to share your viewpoint during a difference of opinion without you being perceived by others as attempting to impose your view as the group's position. This is an important point that I had to learn. The idea of putting someone else first so that others can be heard is totally contrary to the world's way of thinking. If you don't believe me, attend any meeting from Congress down to a neighborhood board. You will find individuals with different opinions. And each one is jockeying for position to be the chief speaker. This spirit of selfishness even blows over into our church meetings. We cut others off and monopolize the floor, and in doing so, we never listen to anyone else. Most of the time, when we are quiet, we are not listening. We are just thinking of what we want to say next. In doing so, we are not acting with respect, love, and humility. We are only acting in selfishness and pride. Selfishness and pride are two traits of the flesh that every Christian should be actively rooting out of their character.

We are also setting a good example to the others when we promote leadership. Jesus taught that if anyone wants to be a leader, he needs to be a servant. Jesus acted this out by washing His disciples' feet (John 13). He was in essence teaching that the way up in the kingdom is down. He was teaching all leadership that if we humble ourselves and promote others, not only will everyone else benefit, but we ourselves will also benefit. The younger saints will learn by our example and will put it to practice in their own churches as well as the Bible study. In the long run, promoting the plurality of leadership produces happy, well run Bible studies that have leaders with servants' hearts. This hinders arguments and promotes the exchange of good ideas and unity. The Bible teaches that there is safety in a multitude of counselors (Proverbs 11:14).

In conclusion, Bible studies at the workplace have the potential of being great avenues of spiritual growth, comfort, protection, healing, learning and unity in the body. They are not only beneficial for the individual who attends but also for our churches in the long run. There may be potential problems that I have not covered with workplace Bible studies, but I strongly feel that the advantages outweigh the possible disadvantages by a thousand to one. There is not a single thing pertaining to this life that does not involve risks. But we should never allow the fear of what might go wrong to keep us from participating in something that has the possibilities of promoting love within the family of God and presenting a unified witness to our unbelieving co-workers.

Chapter 5

Integrity

If we are to have an effective witness for Christ on our jobs, we must be known for our integrity. Integrity is birthed in time of peace and showcased during time of adversity. For us, integrity and godly character must be synonymous terms. We do not gain integrity during hard times because hard times only expose what is already there.

Integrity starts with a commitment of ones will, dreams, and desires to the Lord. Making a commitment during times of adversity is like trying to build shelter during a hurricane. I have told a number of non-believers that they had better make their commitment to Christ now because it will be a lot harder to do it during the time of the Great Tribulation. This thought is true for believers also. We must make our commitment to live godly while we still have times of relative peace to give our integrity a chance to grow and develop a firm foundation.

During times of adversity we act on instinct. By this I mean that we will do what comes natural to us when we are in a crisis situation. It is said that you can raise a skunk from birth along side kittens. You can brush it, groom it, give it all the love it needs, but in a time of crises it is going to act like a skunk. This is why I tell Christians to stop wasting their time preaching to unbelievers about outward acts. What do you expect sinners to act like? They are going to act like sinners because it is their nature. You commonly express what is already within.

In order for integrity to come out during times of adversity, it must already be in us, and it must be our first nature. During a tense situation, we will not have the time to think about what to do. We must act instinctively. For example, when a quarterback throws a pass during a football game and four to six 300-pound man-eating giants come to tackle him, he must act on instinct because he does not have the time to make out a list of all the things he has to do. He does not have the time to stop and say to himself, "well, ok, I'm in a tight spot, I must first make sure I have the ball, next I must align the ball so that the stitches are between my fingers, now I must move my left foot back, now my right, now the left again, now the right. Ok, now what's next? Oh yea! I must bring my arm with the ball back behind my right ear, look down field to find a guy with the same color jersey as mine, move my right arm forward in the directions of the man with the same color jersey, let go of the ball, and hope I live to throw again."

Temptations and trials come at us in the same way. They give us little time to think. This is why we must have the mind of Christ. We must have a made up mind. We must establish in our own hearts that God's way is the only way, and that there are no options or alternatives. Compromise that would adversely affect our integrity is totally out of the question. Such a compromise would lower us from our heavenly place in Christ. Our standards must never be lowered, but we must always rise to the standard and be ready to lift others up also.

To keep from compromising our integrity, we must decide where to draw the line. By this I mean that we must decide ahead of time what we will and will not do. This way we are not as likely to be caught off guard in most circumstances. Romans 12:1 and 2 tell us not to be like the people of the world, but let the Word of God transform how we think. The worldly are always trying to mold us into their image. In many businesses, this is done by pressure and by heat. For example, our boss says, "We must have your results by tomorrow (heat)." "If we don't, you will lose your job (pressure)." To handle the pressure and heat, our minds must be renewed.

What we need is a total brainwashing. A computer can only do what it has been programmed to do. It will not do anything that it does not have a program for. In the same way, we must use God's word to totally erase the old programs that were put in by the world and put God's program in. If the old program has been totally erased, no matter how much pressure or heat is put upon us, we will not do evil because we do not have a program for it. The devil could not get Jesus to compromise his integrity. Jesus says in John 14:30, "hereafter I will not talk much with you for the prince of this world cometh, **and hath nothing in Me**." The devil could not get Jesus to do evil because there was not a program in Jesus to do evil.

Another thing that helps us to maintain integrity is to let others know what your position is "up front." This is particularly important when you start a new job. You can even let your position be known as early as your first job interview. I believe that most interviewers appreciate this approach. If you let the proper people know ahead of time what your conscience will and will not allow you to do, they are less likely to place you in a position which has the possibility of compromising your stand. We must use wisdom in our dealings. I believe that 90 percent of living upright before the Lord is being where He wants us to be and when He wants us to be there.

For instance if there is a position which would cause you to have to work every Sunday morning and your stand is that you go to church on Sunday mornings, the best thing to do would be to not apply for that position. My personal stand is that I will be with God's people on Sunday mornings; therefore, I will not apply for any job that would set me up for conflict. It is absurd to accept a job and pray that the company's scheduling policies change so that you can keep a clear conscience. All of my secular career, I have dealt with scientific data. This data is the evidence that I use to draw conclusions. There are many in the scientific community who will alter or ignore certain data that disagrees with their preconceived notions. This is dishonest and should never be done, but it is commonly done in the secular world. We should not be shocked because there are many Christians who do the same thing with the Word of God to support their own pet doctrines. When I last interviewed, I let those who were interviewing me know that whatever results I got from any test would be what I would record. I would not change or alter any data to make it fit.

At one company, I was told to alter some numbers that I had generated during a test and to sign my name to the final report. I was told that there was not enough time to run the test again because someone was waiting for the results. My immediate supervisor told me that the material surely meets specification because after all "people get paid big money to make sure it does." I was told that I either made a mistake or the sampling was not done right. My higher supervisor came in and started in with the same lines. They were very nice at first, but the tone changed from nice to ridicule and then indignation. They implied that I was incompetent among other things. I told them that I was not going to lie for them or anyone else, including myself, and that if they wanted the report to go out their way, they could change the numbers themselves and sign their own names. I never got another promotion out of them, but I did get one from God. I was able to stand during that time of intense pressure because I had a made up mind. I had already determined that I would rather die than tell a lie. If we are going to be a people of integrity, we must commit to doing things God's way, no matter what it may cost us. A righteous man will do the right thing even when it is inconvenient or hurtful.

I am reminded of another time when I had to stand for righteousness. Before I moved from Gardena, California to Richmond, Virginia with my family, we viewed several brochures of apartment complexes and settled on one that met our needs regarding rent and location. We contacted the manager, filled out the appropriate papers, and sent the funds to secure the apartment we had chosen. When we arrived in Richmond, we picked up the keys from the manager and moved in our furniture. Soon after I started my new job, a young black fellow, I will call him Barney, came to see me. He asked me if I had any difficulty acquiring an apartment. I told him that I had not and briefly related my experience to him. He then told me that there were apartment complexes in Richmond that were discriminating against blacks and that he was part of an organization that was working towards eliminating the practice. Because I am black he hoped that I would have an interest in this matter. He then showed me a few brochures with pictures of apartment complexes, whose management had discriminated against blacks. He said that if I had been discriminated against by any of them would I allow his organization to file a lawsuit in my name. I repeated to him that I had no problem finding an apartment and that I would not allow my name to be used for this purpose.

Barney made a telephone call and then asked me if the head of his organization could speak to me. I told this individual the same thing. I then gave the phone back to Barney, and he conversed with the head of his organization. After a short while Barney said to me, "But it's for a good cause, we know that these companies are blatantly discriminating against blacks." I told him that I would not lie for his cause. The next words out of his mouth enraged me. He looked straight at me and said, "Well, maybe your wife will do it. Can I ask her?" I am not sure what I told him next, but you can be sure that it was not something I could use for the next testimonial service. At that point it would not have hurt me one bit if he did not make it through the "pearly gates."

Barney and his organization's philosophy bare the common misconception of a sin-sick world. This philosophy says that the ends justify the means. I believe that the ends only justify the means if the means are as just as the ends. This is the exact same idea that the serpent used to deceive Eve with- in the Garden of Eden. Let us consider the story found in Genesis 3:1-6:
1 Now the serpent was more crafty than any of the wild animals the LORD God had made. He said to the woman, "Did God really say, 'You must not eat from any tree in the garden'?"
2 The woman said to the serpent, "We may eat fruit from the trees in the garden,
3 But God did say, 'You must not eat fruit from the tree that is in the middle of the garden, and you must not touch it, or you will die.'"
4 "You will not surely die," the serpent said to the woman.
5 "For God knows that when you eat of it your eyes will be opened, and you will be like God, knowing good and evil."

6 When the woman saw that the fruit of the tree was good for food and pleasing to the eye, and also desirable for gaining wisdom, she took some and ate it. She also gave some to her husband, who was with her, and he ate it.

The serpent planted in Eve's mind that the end justifies the means if the ends are fair ends. The serpent convinced Eve that God was not fair in withholding something as important as the "knowledge of good and evil," and therefore she had the right, and even the obligation, to disobey God (means) to correct this abuse and disparity of "informational wealth" (ends). At that point Eve did not take into consideration that disobeying God would not glorify God. In 1Corinthians 10:31, Paul puts it this way. "So whether you eat or drink or whatever you do, do it all for the glory of God." Immoral means do not give God glory. In order for the end result to be right, the process has to be right. In order for the process to be right, the steps of the process must be right.

On biblical principle, I am against the present concepts of Affirmative Action. It is immoral to discriminate against one to make up for discrimination against another, unless the one was the cause of that discrimination. In simpler terms, "Two wrongs do not make a right." I do not believe that the early civil rights leaders suffered what they did to replace the discrimination of one group with the discrimination of another group. Eventually, the tares of the wrong will choke out the fruit of the right, and the end will be worse than the beginning. In my opinion, we just need to do what is right and the fruit of right will overtake the tares of the wrong.

You would think that I had lost whatever chance I had to have Barney hear my witness for Christ, but this was not the case. Because of the stand I took, I believe that I gained credibility. Years latter he told me that he respected and trusted me. I believe that the seeds of that trust were planted that first day we met when I made a righteous stand. For witness sake, it is better for those of the world to hate you and trust you than for them to love you and not trust you. If the worldly do not trust you, they will not trust what you say, and if they do not trust what you say, how will you convince them that Jesus is the Truth?

If we wish to be effective witnesses for Christ, we must present to the world something worth dying for. I believe that if something is worth living for, it is also worth dying for. We must maintain our integrity. Proverbs 11:3 says, "The integrity of the upright guides them, but the unfaithful are destroyed by their duplicity." We must allow our light to shine before the world by our good works so that they can say, "Surely, these are people of God."

Chapter 6
Evangelism

Jesus said in Mark 16:15 that we are to preach the gospel to every creature. In other words, we are to evangelize. We are to tell others of the good news of Jesus Christ. As I said in chapter 1, we Christians that work on secular jobs have the greatest opportunities to evangelize to non-believers because we share the same space for 40 hours or more a week. I certainly have had many opportunities on most of my secular jobs to witness to non-believers. In this chapter, I share with you what I have learned about how, as well as when and where to evangelize.

How to Evangelize on the Job

Based on my personal experiences and knowledge of the Bible, I am convinced that there is no such thing as "the way" to witness on the job. From my search through the scriptures, I have not found any two cases of evangelism that were exactly the same. Even though the central message was always the same in each case, the techniques used to present the gospel varied. This was even true when the gospel was presented by the same evangelist. For example, Paul often used those things that were common to the people he was speaking to as a springboard for sharing the gospel. Once while in Athens, he quoted the inscription on a pagan object of worship to stimulate interest in the gospel (Acts 17:16-34). While the way we evangelize might differ from situation to situation, the paramount message has to be the same: Jesus is the name "under heaven given among men, whereby we must be saved" (Acts 4:12).

While I do not believe there is only one particular way to evangelize on the job, I believe there are some things that we need to consider to help us be more effective when we are witnessing. For example, our lifestyle should be holy. Our lives are living epistles that are read of all who come in contact with us. We cannot live like the devil's children and expect unbelievers to take what we have to say about Jesus seriously. For too long, unbelievers have seen too many hypocritical Christians. The Lord says, "Be holy because I am holy" (I Peter 1:16). The devil has deceived some of us into thinking that holiness is a requirement for preachers only. But, there is only one standard. The Bible says, "Without holiness, no man shall see God" (Matthew 5:8). Without us living holy lives, the world will never see God because the only true God they will see in this life is the one that shines forth from our lives.

When our lifestyle lines up with our talk, we earn the right to share the gospel with our co-workers. They might not like us, they might try to belittle us, they might even threaten to harm us, but if our lives say that we are doing what God wants us to do, most of them will respect us for our strong convictions. I have been asked a number of times by unbelievers, "You mean to tell me that I am going to hell if I don't believe in your Jesus?" I promptly tell them "Yes!" We cannot be frightened by people who will try to make us feel narrow-minded. We must attempt to show them that there is a basket in which they can place all of their eggs. I have found that many unbelievers do not have anything that they can truly believe in. They are looking for something that is sure and secure. We need to show them to the "Rock." However, we will never be able to do so if we do not have their respect.

Another thing that aids our witnessing to our co-workers is our willingness to listen to them. Most people do a lot of talking, but do very little listening. James 1:19 says, "Wherefore my beloved brethren, let every man be swift to hear and slow to speak." This might be why the Lord gave us two ears and only one mouth. Everyone has the need to be heard and to be understood. We all want to feel that what we have to say and what we feel are important to someone. People pay large sums of money to psychologists so that they can be heard. People go to bars because they feel that it is a place to vent their problems to someone who will listen. It is a pity that they do not have the same confidence in our churches. People, in general, do not have the need to be agreed with as much as to know that someone is listening.

Many of us are so concerned about finishing our Christian "sales pitch," that we forget about the needs of the person we are speaking to. We do not hear what they are saying because we are too busy trying to think of what we are going to say next. When we boil everything down, we are being rude and disrespectful. We must always remember that even non-believers are due the respect of a human being who was created in the image of God. I have found that if a person feels that you are honestly listening, they will listen to what you have to say. So what if you have to listen to them for 30 minutes? You just need 5 minutes to give them the gospel. It should not be our goal to get equal time. The goal is to present the gospel to the lost in a clear and precise way.

A major theme in the scripture is the giving up of our rights. This includes any right that we might feel that we have to be heard first or even to have the last word. We are followers of Jesus, who gave up His rights so that man might be saved. Paul wrote in Philippians 2:5-7, "Your attitude should be the same as that of Christ Jesus: Who, being in the very nature of God, did not consider equality with God something to be grasped, but made Himself nothing, taking the very nature of a servant, being made in human likeness."

Jesus gained all because He first gave up all. We must be humble enough to listen and gain understanding before we speak. Most non-believers have a false concept of the gospel. Most non-believers when asked what they must do to be saved mention one or more of the following: You must go to church. You must read the Bible. You must give money to the church. You must help the poor. You must love everybody, and you must, by all means, be good. They also give a list of "thou shall nots." Thou shall not smoke, drink, dance, play pool, cards, or bingo. Thou shall not go to movies, go to parties, chase women, chew gum, curse, and wear pants or makeup, and above all, thou shall not have any fun.

I rarely hear anything about Jesus or His resurrection. This is to the shame of the church. The devil's public relations people have really out done us. To counter their work, we must be willing to find out where a person is coming from so we can address their questions and objections to the gospel. We must not resort to yelling and screaming. Remember we are still on our jobs. Besides, "the wrath of man does not work the righteousness of God" (James 1: 20). We should be swift to hear. Remember, God gave us two ears and only one mouth.

Where and When to Witness

As holy men and women on secular jobs, we need to be mindful that we are always fulfilling two responsibilities. One is to serve the company or organization we work for by being diligent workers for the pay we are receiving. The other is to be light bearers of God's kingdom. Jesus calls us to render unto Caesar the things that are Caesar's and unto God the things that are God's. It is wrong to do anything that disrupts the operation of the company that employs us. The "anything" includes sharing our faith. So if witnessing stops or slows our work or that of another employee, we are in the wrong. I think we all can probably look back to a time or two when we used company time to preach to someone. When we boil everything down, we are stealing time from the company. We are being paid to work for that company, not to witness.

Too many Christians have been fired from their jobs because they decided to use their workplace as a pulpit rather than do their job. When they were confronted about using company time for things other than what they were being paid for, they were quick to proclaim that they were being persecuted for the sake of the gospel. I call it a "martyrdom syndrome." God calls it slothfulness and sin. I Timothy 6:1 says, "Let as many servants as are under the yoke count their own masters worthy of all honor, that the name of God and His doctrine be not blasphemed"(KJV). Many employers have spoken against God because of irresponsible saints who chose to preach rather than to do what they were being paid to do.

When can we share our faith? The primary times for sharing our faith are before the working hours, at breaks, during lunch time, and after hours. I used the words "primary times" because God is not bound by time. God can make time where there is no time when He wants you to witness to someone, and He will make the time for you to witness without you stealing it from the company. To know when God is making the time requires you to be sensitive to the leading of the Holy Spirit. Being sensitive to the Holy Spirit only comes by personally knowing the voice of God as He speaks to our hearts and that only comes by spending time with Him in prayer and meditating on His Word.

Beyond the times stated, there are brief periods of time on the job when circumstances play out to open up doors to evangelize. At some jobs, it may be a computer terminal that has gone down at which time there may be nothing else to do but wait for it to come back up. Another example might be during a fire drill as you are standing outside your workplace. Think of the possibilities with this occasion! On one occasion, I was driving back from an assignment with a fellow worker. The drive back was a perfect opportunity to share Jesus with him since he could not run anywhere and because I could not be accused of wasting company time. You see, it did not prevent or slow either one of us from doing our job. On another occasion, a co-worker and myself had to wait for someone at a cemetery. That was one that I could not pass up. We must always be aware of opportunities. Some jobs have more of a relaxed environment than others in which free conversation is allowed as long as the work gets done. You must know your own situation and allow the Holy Spirit to lead you.

Before ending the chapter, I want to tell you that the Christmas season is a great time for sharing our faith while on the job. If we are observant, God will show us many opportunities. I believe that people's hearts are softer during this season and they are more willing to listen. They tend to be more emotional and sentimental, and since Christ is still part of the topic of the season, we can tell the Christmas story without sounding like we are preaching. On my secular jobs, I love to share the Christmas story and add the salvation message to it. I have found that many people are tired of the commercialization of the season. They want something more fulfilling than what Madison Avenue has to offer. Even those who are not Christians know that there is something wrong with what they see during this holiday. When people express this thought, the time is right to tell them the true meaning of Christmas. We can even quote from Christmas carols that speak of Christ's coming.

I have played the flute for most of my life and I am accomplished enough to play for both the enjoyment of myself and others. I love to play just as much when I am by myself as when I am playing for others. For me, it is an act of worship because I play unto the Lord. I have had the opportunity to entertain at a number of company Christmas parties. The Lord used something that he had given me to give to others so that his kingdom might spread into the secular work place. Many people have spoken to me afterwards about how much they enjoyed my playing which gave me the opportunity to share about the Lord. I have had people talk with me weeks after the event. I have even had people approach me who were either a former employee or the spouse of a former employee. I was recently approached by someone who worked in a totally different part of the company who happened to be in the area. In my conversation with this person, I was able to encourage them in their faith. What I am expressing is, we need to use what we have been given and apply it to our present circumstance to do the King's business.

It is well known that advertisers use melodies and songs to relay their messages to the public. The devil knows this, too. This is why he has made every effort to make sure that Christmas carols are not sung in our public schools and other public places. We have a great opportunity to keep God in the minds of non-believers by singing Christmas carols. Once they get the music of a carol into their heads, they will sometimes hum the tune without consciously knowing it. They might just be humming the tune, but in their heads, they will be putting the lyrics to it and seeds will be sown. So get into the Christmas spirit and sing!

Chapter 7
Persecution

If you are a Christian who is a doer of God's word and not a hearer only, you can expect persecution and suffering on and off the job. I tell you from personal experience that persecution and suffering are never pleasant, and they can be a source of total destruction of your Christian witness. The way we handle them can impact our witness to the unbeliever. Remember, we represent God in the eyes of this world. We are his ambassadors in this world. 2 Corinthians 5:20 says, "We are therefore Christ's ambassadors, as though God were making His appeal through us. We implore you on Christ's behalf: Be reconciled to God." To properly represent Him, we must act as He acted, speak as He spoke, live as He lived, and respond as He responded. Jesus is our example when it comes to overcoming the struggles of this life. He has called us to be more than conquerors through Him who loves us.

Jesus tells us to expect persecution and suffering if we are going to live for Him in this world. In John 15:20, Jesus said, "Remember the words I spoke to you: 'No servant is greater than his master.' If they persecuted Me, they will persecute you also." Peter re-emphasized Jesus' thought on persecution and suffering by saying, "Dear friends, do not be surprised at the painful trial you are suffering, as though something strange were happening to you" (1 Peter 4:12).

The Source of Persecution

Why do you think the Scriptures warn us to expect persecution? It is because we must be alert to the tricks of the devil, our arch enemy. He is the source of all persecution. He is the author of confusion and the enemy of all that is good. If we are going to properly deal with persecution, we must come to grips with Ephesians 6:12: "For our struggle is not against flesh and blood, but against the rulers, against the authorities, against the powers of this dark world and against the spiritual forces of evil in the heavenly realms." If we miss this cornerstone of truth, we will not be effective in our Christian witness when persecution comes. The Bible teaches that God is Spirit (John 4:24) and therefore our dealings with Him must be spiritual. The Devil is also a spirit, and we must also deal with him spiritually. There is no way you can knock the Devil out of someone anymore than you can beat him out of yourself. You cannot fight in the physical realm and expect a victory in the spirit realm. For this reason, we must not only be aware that we will face some degree of persecution in life, including on our jobs, but we must grow in the knowledge of how the realm of the spirit functions. Then by the training of the Holy Spirit, we will be able to overcome the works of the Devil.

From my observations, there are basically four different sources of which the Devil channels persecution through. These can be clearly seen in scripture. They are unbelievers, religious people, rebellious sheep, and direct demonic activity (of which I include false religions).

We will always have persecution from unbelievers for a number of reasons. We are the light of the world (Matthew 5:14), and our light was made to illuminate dark places. This irritates unbelievers because "men love darkness rather than light, because their deeds are evil" (John 3:19). In general, men have done their evil deeds in secret or behind closed doors or in the dark. A life that is consecrated to God uncovers sin and brings conviction. It magnifies and highlights the sin in people's lives. It is as if the unbeliever is looking at his horrid state in a mirror. He wants to see beauty and splendor, but all he sees is filthy rags, and he smells the stench of a rotting carcass. This is why Christians are hated by the world. We do not even have to open our mouths. Our lives bring conviction.

You can often define what something is by saying what it is not. Our holy lifestyle should do the same. It should define who we are in Christ Jesus. The Bible says, "And when He, the Holy

Spirit, is come, He will convict the world of sin, and of righteousness, and of judgment" (John 16:8). We ought to be so full of the Spirit of God that our mere presence brings convictions. We cannot allow unbelievers to be totally comfortable in our presence. I have had many experiences of walking into a room where perverse talk or gossip was going on and just because of my presence the room suddenly turned silent. This is not because of me, but because God entered the room. When I came into the room, I brought God with me. The Holy Spirit is still convicting of sin (John 8:16).

Unbelievers will hate you because we are at war with their monarch. The Devil is the prince of this world (2 Corinthians 4:4 and John 12:31), and unbelievers are his subjects. Jesus made an interesting statement when He was before Pilate. In John 18:36, Jesus told Pilate, "If My kingdom were of this world, then would My servants fight that I should not be delivered to the Jews." In the same way, Satan's servants fight to prevent the conquest of this world system and of its ruler. The people of this world are pawns in the hands of the devil and therefore unknowingly serve him.

Paul said in Romans 8:7, "The sinful mind is hostile towards God." Because of this hostile mindset, we will face persecution. Jesus was persecuted by Herod (Luke 23:1-12) and unmercifully beaten by the Roman soldiers (Mark 15:15-23). He was mocked by the soldiers and the common Jew alike, when He hung on the cross (Mark 15:24-32). Paul was persecuted for his faith in Jesus by unbelievers and finally martyred. Righteous Abel was persecuted by Cain (Hebrews 11:4), Zechariah by the Pharisees (Matthew 23:35), Joseph by Potipher's wife (Genesis 39), Shadrach, Meshach and Abednego by King Nebuchadnezzar (Daniel 3) and all of the Old Testament prophets suffered persecution. If we live for God, we will also be attacked, for all those who live godly *shall* suffer persecution (2 Timothy 3:12).

Another source of persecution, and probably the most severe, is from those I call religious people. These are the group of people who Jesus had the most conflict with. They are the ones who believe they have gotten all that they need to have from God; therefore, they do not need to keep seeking Him. They are the self-righteous, meaning their ways are right in their own eyes. In general, they do not share their faith, and they certainly do not want you to speak to them about yours. They make statements like, "My faith is between me and God and is none of your business. If they want to know about Christianity, they will come to you. If they're really interested, they will come to church on their own." They view any attempt to share the gospel as "ramming religion down someone's throat." They consider themselves to be broad-minded, but they are too narrow-minded to accept your position or even to allow it the right to exist.

They view the scripture through glasses of self-righteousness that carefully screen out anything dealing with a personal relationship with God. They have a form of godliness, but deny the true source of power (2 Timothy 3:5). They are always on the side of the critics of righteousness. They are always ready to stone the spiritual life out of any move of God. They generally go to church every Sunday, but are vehemently opposed to the message of the Gospel or they think that the message applies to others and not themselves. They can take their religion off and put it back on as they please or as any particular circumstance dictates. They have rules and regulations that bind people rather than set them free. They filter the Word of God through the grid of their personal doctrines, opinions, and traditions.

Most of them believe in the "gospel of works" rather than the true gospel of grace. This group, above all others mentioned, believes that they are okay, which makes them the hardest group to reach. It truly takes a mighty move of God's Spirit to break down their fortified walls of self-confidence and hypocrisy. This group will set you up and turn you over to the "Romans" to have you crucified. I believe that this is the group that Jesus referred to in John 16:2 when He said, "They will put you out of the synagogue; in fact, a time is coming when anyone who kills you will think he is offering a service to God."I would advise anyone who is reading this book to never confide in them. If you do, you will live to regret it. I would advise you to walk in love and pray that their spiritual eyes be opened.

The next group that the devil channels persecution through is rebellious sheep. This group can also be broken down into two categories: (1) stray sheep/backslidden Christians and (2) carnal Christians. There are, however, areas where these two categories overlap. You can never backslide without first being carnal. On the other hand, you cannot be carnal without backsliding away from God's best for your life.

A perfect example of the backslider in the Bible is King Saul (1 Samuel Chapters 11-31). He persecuted David, who was an example of a spirit-filled Christian. Saul had strayed so far away from God that he was totally irrational in all of his dealings. I have never known any stray Christians who acted rationally. They tend to do foolish things. They act on impulse. They do not think decisions through. They are very insecure and suspicious. They are never comfortable in a committed Christian's presence. They are uncomfortable because they are running away from the God who that Christian brings with him.

Saul tried to pin David to the wall with his spear (1 Samuel 18:10-16). I have had backsliders try to pin me to a wall with lies and vague accusations. In a certain sense, a part of them loves to have you around, but the other part of them hates you. I have found them to be very unpredictable. You always need to be prayed up when you are around them because they are capable of great mood changes. One minute they love you, and the next, they will attack you with all the fury of hell.

David ministered to Saul by playing his harp, but without warning, Saul tried to kill the person who was trying to help him (1 Samuel 19:8-10). When you minister to a backslider, you will always run the risk of being the object of their fears. A stray sheep will often try to bite the shepherd who is trying to save his life. However, we must always remember not to take their attacks personally. Many times when we are attacked, we will attack back.

This only makes the situation worse. We must be like David who never attacked Saul, but allowed God to fight his battles.

Leading a stray sheep back to the fold is a great opportunity for personal growth. "Brethren, if one of you should wander from the truth and someone should bring him back, remember this: Whoever turns a sinner away from his error will save him from death and cover many sins" (James 5:19-20). This is not an easy task, but contrary to Cain's opinion, we are our brother's keeper (Genesis 4:1-15). We must also restore in love, meekness, and humility.

The rebellious sheep group tends to contain wounded sheep. They have been wounded by other sheep and shepherds. When one of our own has been wounded, we too often pour salt in their wounds or shoot them. Generally, what occurs is that the wounded sheep will outwardly blame others, but this is a cover. Who they really blame, deep down inside, is God. They blame God for their problems, and they do not have the courage to admit it to others or even to themselves. So they subconsciously say to God, "I gave you a chance, but you blew it." At this point they keep God at arms length and do not allow Him to come close enough to hurt them again. They also include anyone who represents God by word or deed.

The interesting thing is that you will not receive any persecution from the rebellious sheep as long as you keep your distance. To reach this group you must combine love with good old-fashion tenacity. You must determine in your mind that you will never give up on them until they have come back to God. This does not necessarily mean to badger them, but it does mean to take every opportunity that you are allowed by them to minister God's love and forgiveness. Sometimes you will have to back off for a while, but backing off should never include giving up. It means waiting for the Lord to open doors. We do not need to try to make the openings. We just need to go through the openings when they present themselves. Many times the openings will have jagged edges; so there will be times when we will receive scratches, abrasions, and cuts. However, we must keep our eyes on the goal, the restoration of a soul. We must always go in a spirit of meekness. You will never be able to beat sheep back into the fold. They must first learn to trust you and feel assured in themselves that you have a good honest concern for them without any ulterior motive. Once this happens, you can lead them back to the fold.

Carnal Christians have many of the traits of backslidden Christians. They go to church, hear the Word of God preached, listen to Christian radio, and watch Christian television, but they have at sometime in their Christian walk stopped growing. They are content with "spiritual milk" and have not pressed into the deeper things of God. They have been in the faith for 5, 10, 20 or 50 years, but they refuse to grow up. They are motivated by feelings and emotions. Paul wrote a lengthy letter to a carnal church at Corinth. In this letter he admonishes that church for being worldly. "Brothers, I could not address you as spiritual but as worldly – mere infants in Christ. I gave you milk, not solid food, for you were not yet ready for it. Indeed, you are still not ready. You are still worldly. For since there is jealousy and quarreling among you, are you not worldly? Are you not acting like mere men?" (1 Corinthians 3:1-3).

Carnal Christians love to here and even talk about the things of God. They love to quote scripture and sing gospel songs. They even love to tell you what God has done for them. They are chasing after everything the world is chasing after. Their hearts are a cross between the rocky shallow ground and the field that was full of thorns. They are shallow and materialistic. These are the ones that Jesus referred to in the letter to the church at Laodicea in Chapter 3 of the Book of Revelation. They are neither hot nor cold. They have convinced themselves that they have everything together and do not need anymore of God. They are the ones to whom Jesus is knocking on the door of their hearts and calling for them to answer.

Carnal Christians will often side with unbelievers against you. They look at the moral failings of a leader and say, "Nobody is perfect." They are willing to overlook sin in the public sphere as well as in the Church. Their motto is, "Thou shalt not judge." They are willing to forgive everyone except those who would have the audacity to cry out against sin. They are the ones who try to walk as close to the world as possible. By their lives, you will have a difficult time distinguishing them from unbelievers. They talk like them, act like them, and live like them. Their conversation and point of view are worldly. They gossip, curse, sleep around, get drunk, lie, and watch totally ungodly movies. They also have no problem listening to anyone consistently use profane language while at the same time they shudder when you speak about righteousness and God's standards for living.

This group mainly persecutes you by their words to unbelievers. They try to make you look like an extremist, not in the "main stream." You are a fanatic, a right-wing religious zealot and a narrow-minded bigot. I have probably received more criticism from this group than any other group. Unfortunately, the world views this group as being the true representation of the Church. Whenever the world wants to bash the Church, it can always find some carnal Christian to back them up. It generally takes something catastrophe in the lives of carnal Christians to turn them around. As in the case of the backslider, we must pray that God will open their eyes and give us an opening to reach them.

I have stated that the fourth source of persecution the Devil uses is demonic activity. However, I do not believe it is the Devil persecuting you every time something bad happens to you. However, I do believe that if you serve God fervently enough and long enough, you will experience some form of demonic persecution.

It may come through other employees. It may come in the form of depression or sickness. It may come in the form of evil thoughts or temptation. It may come in the form of condemnation. All of these things are for the purpose of sidetracking the saints of

God from doing the work He has called us to do. If you are doing enough damage to the kingdom of darkness, do not fool yourself into believing that the Devil is just going to sit still and take it. He will do his best to neutralize you and destroy your witness. However, we do have a promise from God that will help us overcome Satan's attacks. It is found in James 4:7, "Submit yourselves then to God. Resist the Devil, and he will flee from you." The key is submitting to God. Without submission to the Lord, we cannot resist the Devil's attacks. If we cannot resist his attacks, why should he flee? No army runs away if it is meeting only limited resistance. When we are under spiritual attack, we need to be as close to God as we can be. This means submission to His will.

We must also make sure we have the whole armor of God on us before we arrive at work. This means that we must spend time with our Commander and Chief to receive instructions before we arrive on the job. This is also a good time to reaffirm our dependency on God and also to recommit our wills to Him. Ask God to lead you. Ask Him to sharpen your spiritual senses. Ask Him to allow you to see the people at your place of employment through His eyes. Ask Him to give you a discerning spirit so that you can differentiate between good and evil as well as truth from error. Ask Him to protect you as well as your fellow Christians who are on your job. God's armor has been provided for us to withstand the attacks of the enemy and having withstood all, we will stand (Ephesians 6:10-18). (For additional comments about demonic persecution see Chapter 7--Bible Study.)

Reacting to Persecution

Before I close this chapter, I want to touch on a different aspect of persecution. It is how we react to the persecution the Devil brings our way. Jesus taught in his Sermon on the Mount to "Love your enemies, and pray for those who persecute you" (Matthew 5:44). These commands are so foreign to our sinful nature that many have denied the literal acceptance of this scripture. I feel that there are two main reasons for Jesus making these commands.

The first is to maintain our communion with God. We need to maintain a right heart attitude if we are going to reap the blessings of God. God works through love and faith. When we have hatred and bitterness in our hearts, which can be byproducts of persecution if we do not obey God's instruction, we block our communion with Him.

Hatred is evil. God is love (1 John 4:8-9). Evil and darkness are synonymous in the Bible. People who are full of hate are full of darkness, which prohibits the presence of God. God does not cohabitate with sin and darkness. When we hold hatred in our hearts we are like a branch that is cut off from the vine, Christ that cannot bear fruit (John 15:1-2). This fruit includes the harvesting of souls. We must keep our hearts in the love of God.

Man was not created to carry hatred and bitterness in his heart. They have a way of destroying people's relationships, even relationships with those that they love. Hatred and bitterness eat away at your spirit, soul, and body. A person who is consumed with hatred and bitterness does not think logically. He is not as productive as he can be. He does not learn as much. He does not have inner peace because the peace of God is not inside. We were created to live in peace. We are at our best when we are at peace. This is why David said in the 23rd Psalm "He leads me beside the still waters" (verse 2).

Our bodies are not designed to carry hatred and bitterness. I have heard that some sickness can be traced back to unforgiveness, which is hatred and bitterness that is not released. Hatred causes chemical imbalances in our bodies. It produces excess acid in our stomachs and intestines that cause ulcers. It makes our blood pressure rise to unhealthy levels and puts extra stress on our hearts. It causes certain cancers. This is interesting because hatred and bitterness eat away at a person's spirit while ulcers and cancers eat away at the physical body. Jesus came that we might have life and that more abundantly (John 10:10). Harbored hatred brings death because death is the wages of sin (Romans 6:23). We defeat the purpose of Christ if we do not deal with hatred.

Jesus teaches us to deal with hatred by nipping it in the bud. We must destroy the seeds before they can take root in our hearts. The principle is the same for other sins also. Temptation will always come. You cannot stop a thought from coming, but you can keep it from taking up residence and becoming a shareholder in your decision-making. The strategy is to keep the seeds of hatred and bitterness from germinating inside of us. The longer we allow those thoughts to stay inside of us, the deeper the roots go. Jesus was trying to teach us that time has an important part to play. He is saying that we must act immediately. Most seeds are small and are hardly noticeable. They are easily covered up and out of sight. Plants do not pop up until they have established roots. This means that you have to uproot them, which can be painful. If we do not uproot them they will proceed to bear fruit in our lives. If we love our enemies, the seeds of hatred and bitterness are not allowed the time to germinate and grow roots.

In saying that we should love our enemies, Jesus was not saying that we should be close friends with them. Nor is He saying we should be emotionally swayed when we are in the presence of someone who is doing us wrong or despitefully using us. Instead He is teaching us to desire the ultimate good for that person.

I Corinthians13: 5 states that love "thinks no evil." True love does not desire evil to come upon the object of that love.
1 Corinthians 13:7 says love "hopes all things." Love always hopes for the best. Jesus' teachings are very practical. It is impossible to hate a person whose best you are hoping for. I have found it to be very difficult to hold bitterness in my heart against someone who I am earnestly praying for. Praying in humility and honesty always puts our hearts in the right place.

Jesus also says that we are to do good to them that hate us. Proverbs 25:21-22 says, "If your enemy is hungry, give him bread to eat; and if he is thirsty, give him water to drink. For you will heap coals of fire upon his head, and the Lord shall reward you." Giving is love in action. I once heard a preacher say, "If you harbor bad feelings against someone, do something nice for them and watch the change." I decided to try it out one day on a fellow employee who felt that his mission in life was to make me miserable. I must confess that he was making some headway. One day this person forgot to take his jacket home with him. It was at a time when personal items were being stolen after hours. On my way out, I spotted the jacket and locked it away until the next day when I would see him. It was in my power to do good, and I chose to do so. My coworker's attitude changed towards me with this act of kindness. It brought about peace between us. He even began to give me gifts and speak highly of me to his family and others. Proverbs 16:7 says, "When a man's ways are pleasing to the Lord, he makes even his enemies live at peace with him." This coworker and I never became best friends, but there was enough peace for me to live the gospel before his eyes.

One of the most unpleasant situations to be in on a job is to share an office with someone whose worldly ways conflict with your Christian values. Such a situation can be a breeding ground for conflicts that can lead to hatred and bitterness. I experienced such a situation when I was transferred to another department and was assigned to share an office with a man whom I did not know very well. When I entered my new office, I was confronted with a statue of a nude woman on a filing cabinet. It was at almost eye level. There was absolutely no way I could keep from seeing it. I said to myself, "I am not going to come into my office 20 times a day, 5 days a week and be confronted with this statue." I asked my new office mate if he could at least move it to his desk so it would be out of my immediate view. He told me in so many terms that it was out of the question. Upon hearing this, I went to my new supervisor, who is a godly man, and explained the situation and asked if I could be assigned to a different office.

My supervisor, without my knowledge, told my new office mate that he had to move his statue. When I next entered our shared office, he had moved the statue from the cabinet, where it had sat for over a decade, to his desk. As you might have suspected, this did not endear me to him. He told me to never speak to him again along with a few other choice words. To make matters worse, or better depending on your point of view, within a couple of days a woman complained to an upper level manager about some lewd pictures that someone had displayed in her department. This manager then sent a notice to everyone that all sexually explicit paraphernalia were forever banished throughout all of our buildings. Not only did my office mate's statue have to leave the cabinet, it also had to leave the building.

Of course it was noised abroad that I was the "self-righteous religious fanatic" who was imposing his views and forcing his morals down everyone's throat. Do you know what it feels like to be hated and despised by scores of people? The worst of it was I had to face the kingpin of that venom on a constant basis. The air was so thick in our tiny office, that you could cut it with a knife. If looks could kill, someone else would be writing this book because I would be with the Lord by now.

My office mate was clearly wrong. I was clearly right. But I had to remember that I had given up my rights to retaliate when I came to Jesus and proclaimed Him as Lord of my life. I had to do what He called me to do. I had to make every effort to bring peace because that is what all Christians have been called to do. "Blessed are the peacemakers, for they will be called sons of God" (Matthew 5:9). I decided to bless and not curse, love and not hate, speak kindly and not harshly. In other words I decided to act like Jesus. I never stopped saying good morning or acting kindly towards him. May I also say that time is of the essence to do the right thing. The longer you wait to do it, the harder it is. I would go out of my way to give him his phone messages. I would not say negative things about him. This point is very important because if we speak negative things toward someone, we find it harder to release the bitterness. In short, "We have what we say."

The Lord will always act on our behalf when we do things His way. Within a month, the man got a promotion that he had been denied for many years. Upon hearing of it I looked him in the eyes and with sincerity congratulated him for obtaining his goal. He looked at me with a puzzled gaze and choked out the words, "Thank you, Tom." From that time on, his countenance changed towards me and there was peace. I gained a greater understanding of what it means, "In doing this, you will heap burning coals on his head" (Romans 12:20).

In conclusions, we must always remember that if we live for God, we will be persecuted in one way or another. "If we live for God, we will be attacked also because all those who live godly *shall* suffer persecution" (2 Timothy 3:12). This scripture lets us know that we cannot always stop the persecution. However, the way to overcome the persecution is by loving, blessing, praying, walking by faith, submitting to the word of God, and patience.

Chapter 8

Supervisors

An important area of concern for Christians on their jobs is how to relate to their supervisors. It seems that the only bosses we give proper respect to are the overbearing ones. A Christian should never take unfair advantage of a supervisor's meekness or benevolence, but must always give him or her the proper respect. We miss out on a great witnessing opportunity when we do not give our supervisors the proper respect. Ephesians 6:5 might have the best instructions for how we ought to interact with our supervisors. It says, "Slaves, obey your earthly masters with respect and fear, and with sincerity of heart, just as you would obey Christ." The basic principle is give honor to whom honor is due (Romans 13:7).

There has been a swing of the pendulum in our nation from the boss being lord and master of our total lives to him being just one of the boys, or no better than anyone else. On one hand, it is wrong for a supervisor to demean those who they are over and treat them like they are brick-making slaves in ancient Egypt. On the other hand, it is equally as wrong for an employee to go tit for tat in telling the supervisor how things ought to be done or what he will or will not do because that supervisor either does not have the authority to fire them or he is just too timid to do so. I have heard individuals openly defy their supervisors. In essence, they not only defied the one whom they were accountable to, but they were also defying God. I'm not talking about personally standing against sin and unrighteousness that someone over you might attempt to make you take part in. I am referring to the areas where Caesar has jurisdiction. Christians, above all others, need to exemplify obedience in the workplace when the supervisors give instructions that do not violate their faithful conscience. If we do not, I am convinced that God is going to hold us accountable.

We live in an era in this nation in which there is a disintegration of respect for all authority. Many who are now Christians grew up in the 1960's. This time period was marked by slogans that suggested, if not out right stated, that all authority was evil and therefore should not be submitted to or should be ignored and even torn down. The heroes of our society today are the mavericks. They get things done their own way regardless of the wishes of their supervisors. We take great delight in those who break all the rules to get the job done, to catch the bad guys, to shoot down the enemy airplane, to make the winning touch down, to take the winning shot in spite of their coach's instructions. We love to see them achieve the great gain while at the same time making those who have authority over them appear to be inept and stupid.

We do not obey our supervisors because we did not obey our parents, and we have difficulty obeying God. We may not always get the job done right, but we are always paid to carry out the companies' wishes. Once again every Christian needs to render unto Caesar the things that are Caesar's. If we are told by a supervisor to do something a certain way in which we either think that there is either a better way or it cannot possibly work, we need to offer alternatives. If that supervisor still wants us to do it his way, we need to cheerfully and diligently do everything in our power to make his way a shining success. What so often happens is that we mumble and grumble and drag our feet to assure that the bosses' plans are not as productive as they might be. This behavior not only shows a lack of respect, but contempt for our supervisors and God. So let us show proper respect to authority. We give God glory and maintain a good report and witness to this world when we do.

Joseph's Attitude toward Authority

A person in the Scriptures who we can use as an example of how we ought to act toward a supervisor is Joseph. He was a godly young man who had to work in a secular environment with ungodly supervisors. Joseph had brains, position, and power. He also had the confidence and trust of the people of Egypt. He could easily have said to himself, "I am the brains of this operation, and I should be the head instead of Pharaoh." In Genesis 47:25, the Egyptians said, "You have saved our lives. May we find favor in the eyes of our lord; we will be in bondage to Pharaoh." I am sure that at this point because of Joseph's popularity and the admiration of the people he could easily have overthrown Pharaoh. Joseph even managed Pharaoh's household. In Genesis 45:8, Joseph said, "So then, it was not you who sent me here, but God. He made me father to Pharaoh, lord of his entire household and ruler of all Egypt." Yet Joseph never became high minded. He did not rebel or usurp Pharaoh's authority. He remained faithful to the end to his supervisor and allowed the Lord to promote him.

Judging Supervisors Fairly

If we view a situation from our supervisor's perspective, we might willingly obey him. In this self-centered society, we are often so absorbed in our own situation that we forget that others are also going through trials. I have heard Christians, myself being one of them, make the following comments: "They don't care if I don't have enough money to live on. They just want to hoard all the money for themselves. They just don't want me to have anything. They just want to keep me poor." I believe that at least 95 percent of the time these statements are untrue if not outright lies. They are also mostly unfair. If we were truly honest, we would have to admit that our boss really does not want to see us and our families out on Skid Row. They do not want to see any of their employees out on a medium by a stop light and holding a crayon drawn sign that says, PLEASE HELP, I HAVE A FAMILY, WILL WORK FOR FOOD. I have come to learn that at least most of our immediate supervisors would grant any reasonable request if they were able, if for no other reason than to keep peace.

Let me share a personal story. Early in my career, I have had my share of confrontations with my immediate supervisors over my salary. I felt that I deserved to be promoted. However, the motives that I accused my supervisors of for not putting me in for promotions were not always correct. Sometimes I harshly and unfairly judged them. Over the years, I have become aware of important information regarding the decision-making process of large companies. Lower level supervisors rarely have much say when it comes to you getting a raise. If I had known this earlier in my secular career, I would have been more considerate and would have been a better witness for Christ.

Here is how I believe my scenario was played out. I went to my immediate supervisor and gave him my list of reasons for deserving the promotion. That supervisor went to his supervisor who went to his manager. That manager did not personally know me or the quality of my work. That manager told my supervisor's supervisor that my promotion was denied. My immediate supervisor said to him, "I think Tom deserves the promotion." What am I going to tell him? The answer came back, "I don't know, tell him anything."

Now my immediate supervisor has a big problem. He has to come up with something to tell me. He cannot say that he believes I ought to have what I asked for, but upper management said no. So the immediate supervisor ended up giving me vague and abstract or trivial reasons why I did not deserve to be promoted. Such reasons made my immediate supervisor appear heartless and uncaring. I would always push the issue, thus making it more and more difficult for my immediate supervisor. Eventually, this created a poor relationship between my supervisor and me. This totally removed any possibility for me to be an effective witness to him. It is almost impossible to share the gospel of Jesus Christ with a person who believes that your whole reason for existence is to bring trouble into their life.

I have used this personal illustration to show that we need to be a little more patient with our supervisors and to remind us that we need to be careful not to judge others too quickly. We do not know the whole story all the time! Being sensitive to the needs and problems of others, whether fellow employees or our supervisors, will open more doors to share our faith than trying to break the doors down.

Dealing with Unjust Supervisors

The next topic I want to address in this chapter is how should Christian employees handle unjust, unfair, or overbearing supervisors? Just as there are some employees who feel their mission in life is to make you miserable, there will be some supervisors who feel they have that same calling. This is a tough situation for anyone to be in because no one likes to be mistreated or abused. Everyone wants to work in a pleasant environment with pleasant people. No one wants to have anyone "breathing down their back." We all want positive approval for our work. But this will not always be the case. In fact, I believe that God will make sure that this is not always the case. God chooses, at times, to place us in hard situations for our growth and for His glory. This is because God is interested more in our character than in our comfort. In order to accomplish this He will use people as His means to conform us into the image of His Son. "And we know that in all things God works for the good of those who love Him, who have been called according to His purpose" (Romans 8:28).

I searched the scripture to locate the worst possible supervisor and I believe that I have found your worst nightmare. How would you like to work for King Saul? Saul was the CEO of Israel. David was a little shepherd boy who worked for him. He was not even a mailroom clerk in the corporate scheme of things. David was a "nobody" in the eyes of the world, but he did receive good references. If you think you have it bad, David had it worse. The story can be found in Chapter 16 of 1 Samuel. Verses 14 and 15 of that chapter say, "Now the Spirit of the Lord had departed from Saul, and an evil spirit from the Lord tormented him. Saul's attendants said to him, an evil spirit from God is tormenting you."

Have you ever worked for someone who was demon possessed? I have worked for some disgusting people before, but I have never had the misfortune of working for someone who was totally full of the devil. Even though we might say that our supervisor is full of the devil, we do not really mean it. There is a big difference between someone who is mean, nasty, and hard to get along with and someone who is under the control of Satan himself. Though not on a secular job, I have personally had the experience of being confronted by someone in this condition. It can be a scary situation. You never know what to expect. I have also spoken to missionaries who have, and they express the same thing. They were in a life or death situation.

At one point Saul took his javelin and tried to pin David to a wall. Has your supervisor ever attempted to kill you? Even after David quit his job and fled, Saul pursued him for the purpose of taking his life. I want us to note that this persecution was not because David had done something wrong. David was good at his job. He had removed a huge obstacle, Goliath, for the armies of Israel in their battle with the Philistines. He reached into his bag and took out a stone, which he slung and struck the Philistine in the forehead. He killed Goliath, who had fallen facedown on the ground (1 Samuel 7:49). The armies of Israel had stalled. David got them moving again. Everyone spoke well of him. He did not have personnel conflicts. He solved major problems. He was faithful and when he was given an assignment, he accomplished it. According to 1 Samuel 18:5, whatever Saul sent him to do, David did it so successfully that Saul gave him a high rank in the army. This pleased all the people and Saul's officers as well. He was able to take a little and accomplish much.

The reason I have emphasized these scriptures is to show David's response to his extremely difficult situation. In them we have a blueprint of how we ought to live our lives before a harsh supervisor. The first thing to remember is that though we are not always responsible for the actions of others, we are responsible for our own action. Saul was trying to harm David because he was jealous of David (1 Samuel 18:5-12), but David decided to do the right thing by not striking back. There were at least two times when David could have done evil against Saul, but he did not do so. He decided that neither people nor circumstances are justifications to do that which is not right. It was in David's heart to do what was right.

Just as in David's case there will be those who will try to get us to do that which is convenient. David's men thought that killing Saul was a quick fix for David's problem. Somehow we are convinced that if only our supervisors would leave the company everything would be fine. Quick fixes might mask or hide a problem for a while, but they never solve them. If we do not deal with our problems, we will see them again even though they may have a different face or form. If we read to the end of David's story, we will see that David received everything that the Lord had promised him. What God has for you, is for you. It does not matter who stands in your way; if God said it, it will come to pass. The only one that can hinder God's blessing in your life is you! We hinder God when we do not do the right thing.

David did not try to obtain the promises of God in his own way. Too many times we are guilty of trying to obtain God's blessings by our own means. The Bible is full of examples of this. Abraham and Sarah tried to obtain an heir with their own plan (Genesis 16). Jacob tried to steal Esau's birthright (Genesis 25). Saul offered the sacrifice that Samuel was supposed to offer so that his army would be victorious (Genesis 13:5-14). These people were striving by their own means to accomplish something that was already settled. Sometimes we fight battles with our supervisors when the Lord has already given us the victory. Why should Jesus bow down and worship Satan for kingdoms that were going to belong to Him (Matthew 4:8-11)? If Jesus had bowed to Satan, He would have lost the kingdoms of this world. If we bow to our sinful nature and do the wrong thing, we will lose. Remember we are responsible for our own actions.

Additionally, David did not retaliate against Saul. The Bible admonishes us about retaliating. "Do not take revenge, my friends, but leave room for God's wrath, for it is written: It is Mine to avenge; I will repay, says the Lord. On the contrary, if your enemy is hungry, feed him; if he is thirsty, give him something to drink. In doing this, you will heap burning coals on his head. Do not be overcome by evil, but overcome evil with good" (Romans 12:19-21). Nothing should be done for revenge. It is far better to let God handle it. When Abishai wanted to take Saul's life, David had a perfect response.

I Samuel 26:7-10
7 So David and Abishai went to the army by night, and there was Saul, lying asleep inside the camp with his spear stuck in the ground near his head. Abner and the soldiers were lying around him.
8 Abishai said to David, "Today God has delivered your enemy into your hands. Now let me pin him to the ground with one thrust of my spear; I won't strike him twice."
9 But David said to Abishai, "Don't destroy him! Who can lay a hand on the Lord's anointed and be guiltless?
10 "As surely as the LORD lives," he said, "the LORD Himself will strike him; either his time will come and he will die, or he will go into battle and perish."

We are always to do the best job that we can. Too often when employees are in conflict with management, they drag their feet. They do not put out their best effort. They do not seek excellence. They say, "If he is going to treat me this way, I'm not going to break my neck to get this work done." In the passages in I Samuel, it appears that even though King Saul was on David's back, David's job performance did not suffer and in fact it got better. In 1 Sam 18:30, when the Philistine commanders continued to go out to battle, and as often as they did, David had more success than the rest of Saul's officers, and his name became well known. It was during this time that his job accomplishments out shined all the other workers. David diligently served Saul. He was "employee of the year" even in the mist of severe persecution. This is the kind of employee that God wants us to be. He wants us to shine like a lighthouse in the mist of the storm. In the face of adversity, He has ordained that we be "more than conquerors" (Romans 8:37).

We need to remember that ultimately we are serving the Lord. Paul puts it this way, "Whatever you do, work at it with all your heart, as working for the Lord, not for men, since you know that you will receive an inheritance from the Lord as a reward. It is the Lord Christ you are serving" (Colossians 3:23-24). It helps a great deal when we are dealing with unjust supervisors to get our eyes off of them and place our eyes on the Lord. It was when Peter took his eyes off of Jesus that he looked at the waves and the storm and began to sink (Matthew 14:22-31). I believe that many are sinking today into bitterness, anger, despair and hopelessness because they have taken their eyes off of Jesus. Do you have a sinking feeling when you see your supervisor? Has the Saul in your life blotted out the vision of the Lord? Turn your eyes upon Jesus!

We also need to pray for our supervisors. It is hard to remember in the mist of frayed feelings that we need to pray for those who persecute us, but this is the command of God. Paul says, "I urge, then, first of all, that requests, prayers, intercession and thanksgiving be made for everyone, for kings and all those in authority, that we may live peaceful and quiet lives in all godliness and holiness" (I Timothy 2:1). The objective of this admonition is to achieve a "peaceful and quiet life in all godliness and holiness." If this is our goal, we will pray for our supervisors. Remember our mission is to reach everyone we can for Christ, not just the ones that we like. We are not to limit our mission to those who are our peers or those who are at levels beneath us. As I have stated in a previous chapter, it is difficult to reach someone who we are in active conflict. That is why Paul says, "If it is possible, as far as it depends on you, live at peace with everyone" (Romans 12:18). This approach pleases God, and when our ways please Him, He will even cause our enemies to be at peace with us (Proverbs 16:7).

In conclusion, I end this chapter with two scriptures for you to ponder:
1 Peter 2:18   Slaves, submit yourselves to your masters with all respect, not only to those who are good and considerate, but also to those who are harsh.
1 Pet 2:23   When they hurled their insults at Him (Jesus), He did not retaliate; when He suffered, He made no threats. Instead, He entrusted Himself to Him who judges justly.

Chapter 9

Wages

I must confess that the parable in Matthew 20:1-15 about the landowner and hired laborers has never set well with my selfish nature. Nevertheless, I have to accept it for what it says, rather than what I want it to say.

In this parable, the landowner hired the first workers early in the morning. The others were hired at 9 am, noon, 3 pm, and about 5 p.m. Yet, the landowner paid all of them the same amount. Those who worked the longest complained to the landowner because they thought they should have been given more than the others. Here is the landowner's response to one of them, "Friend, I am not being unfair to you. Didn't you agree to work for a denarius? Take your pay and go. I want to give the man who was hired last the same as I gave you. Don't I have the right to do what I want with my own money? Or are you envious because I am generous?"

Before I go any further, let me say that Matthew 20:1-15 is not directly speaking about our wages on the job. Actually, it is teaching that the one who accepts Jesus' invitation at the "eleventh hour" will still make it into the Kingdom of Heaven just like those who have been serving the Lord for most of their lives. The passage also is teaching that salvation is not by works but by grace through faith.

Company's Right to Decide Wages

At this point, I am sure you are saying, "So what is my point for using it if it does not apply to wages?" Bear with me while I answer this question. There is a principle in the question in Matthew 20:15 that strike at the very core of our 21st century American culture. The question is, "Don't I have the right to do what I want with my own money?"

We live in a society that is very selfish. Every thought, desire, dream, and whim is "me," "my," and "I." Our self-worth is tied in with how much we make and how much we have. It is the "Keeping up with the Jones" mentality. We in this nation have gotten so "me and mine" oriented that we subconsciously believe that we own everything. Just listen to the media advertisement clichés. Car commercials imply that if you buy the car being advertised "you own the road." Credit card commercials tell us that in having the advertised card "you possess the world." Graduating classes are told to go out and "conquer the world." Even in many of our churches we are taught that if you want it, praise God, it is yours. I call this teaching the "covet it, claim it" doctrine.

Now let us see how this selfish attitude relates to our wages. I want to begin by saying that I am not addressing whether wages are fair or not. By and large, every wage will never be totally fair as long as we have man in control. What I am addressing is Christians' attitude towards their wages. Our attitudes have to be right before God regardless of what man does or does not do. The Lord is more interested in our attitude towards our wages than our wages. This lesson was one of the hardest for me to learn. I am not saying that I have achieved perfection in this area, but I believe I am headed in the right direction.

I believe we must come back to the realization that unless we are major stockholders, we do not own the company we work for. This might seem like an overly obvious statement, but deep down inside, many of us feel that "the company ought to" or "the company owes me." When you boil everything down, the only time someone owes us something is when that someone has something that personally belongs to you. On the other side of the coin there are companies that believe they own their employees. Both sides are wrong.

Source and Resource of Finances

We who are Christians must come to the realization that God, not the company, is our source of finances. God is our *source* while the company is just a *resource*. This statement might also sound elementary, but I believe that many Christians do not subconsciously make the connection between God being our supplier and our paychecks. Because we do not, we tend to murmur and complain about our salaries. We say things to other employees such as: "They don't pay us anything here. This cheap company.... They don't care anything about me. They only want to keep us down and poor." We start to speak against the vehicle of God's provision in our lives. When we do this, we are actually murmuring against God. Every time we use the word "they" or "them," we are actually saying God. We are saying "God wants to keep us poor. God wants to keep us down. God does not care."

Allow me to use myself as an example. At a prior job I felt that I was not being paid enough for my services. Others were coming in after me with less experience and education and were being paid more. I felt cheated, and I let my company know it. When my cries fell on death ears, I cried even louder and more often. Soon every comment was a complaint about my salary. The sad part is that all of my financial needs were being met. I was not in any financial need at this time. I could not see that God was supplying all of my needs even though I was not getting what I thought was "my just share." I also could not see that just one office level above my supervisor was God, who heard every accusation and complaint. It was not until another Christian, who was younger in the Lord than myself, spoke a word from God to me and said, "You have lost your witness." At that moment I knew how David must have felt when Nathan said to him, "Thou art the man," when he confronted David about the evil he had done (2 Samuel 11:1-12).

That Christian was right. The last few months of my life seemed to have past before my eyes in an instance. I had lost my witness. The unbelievers there could not see Jesus. All they could see was a complainer. No one likes to be around someone who constantly complains. Whether my cause was just or unjust did not seem to matter very much at that point. My so called rights did not amount to a hill of ice in the arctic. What did matter was the image and testimony of He whom I serve. What we need to come to grips with in this "me generation" is that when we come to Jesus, we surrender our pride, selfish desires, will, rights, and dreams. He is "all in all" and He could never be anything less.

Being Content with Our Salaries

Paul said that he had learned to be content in whatever circumstance he was in (Philippians 4:11). This circumstance also applies to our salaries. This is a hard pill to swallow for us in this egotistic society, however, in contentment lies peace and with peace comes joy. Paul is not saying that you should never try to improve your situation or your salary. God wants us to prosper in every area of our lives as our soul prospers (3 John, verse 3). Paul also says in Philippians 4:6 "Do not be anxious about anything." And in Matthew 6:33, Jesus says, "Seek first His kingdom and His righteousness and all these things will be given to you as well." As I mentioned before, during my time of complaining, I did not go lacking. I believe that just as Jesus multiplied the fish and the loaves (Matthew 14:13-21 and 15:32-39) He also made my paycheck stretch. Why should I get so upset for not getting a 5 percent raise when God caused my salary to stretch as far as if I were making 20 percent more?

Always Be Thankful

We also need to always maintain an attitude of thankfulness. For the Christian, everyday ought to be Thanksgiving. When we murmur against our jobs because of our wages, we show ingratitude toward God. We must be thankful for what we have. We are so blessed in this nation! Even the poor in this nation have a standard of living which is higher than most of the world. We could have been born in a place or time when there was terrible oppression, famine, war, slavery, poverty, and fear. I am sure that none of us have gone through what Paul suffered; and yet, there is no record of him ever complaining about his wages. Instead he rejoiced during the hard times and gave God the glory by bringing the sacrifice of praise. Remember "do all things to the glory of God" (1 Corinthians 10:31). It is far better to seek other employment opportunities than to lose our witness by murmuring and complaining every day from 9 to 5 for the rest of our career. Let us learn what Paul learned: ". . . and the peace of God, which transcends all understanding, will guard [our] hearts and minds through Christ Jesus" (Philippians 4:7).

Chapter 10

Controversy

Paul wrote, "Endure hardship with us like a good soldier of Christ Jesus. No one serving as a soldier gets involved in civilian affairs–he wants to please his commanding officer" (2 Timothy 2:3-4). In the New Testament, a Christian is compared to a soldier. We as soldiers must always be prepared to do battle against the "powers of darkness," because our struggle is against the spiritual evil forces of this world. We have been born again to fight spiritual battles. We have been called to advance on the gates of Hell and set the captives free. However, we will not be effective in our fight against these spiritual evil forces if our resources are diverted to areas that do not matter.

Because of the holiness of God and the fallen nature of man, Christians will always have controversy surrounding them. This is because the message of the cross is at odds with sinful man. All of those who we read about in the Bible were at the vortex of controversy. This eventually led to persecution. It seems that everywhere Paul went, trouble broke out. There were riots in Jerusalem and Thessalonica. A riot broke out in Jesus' own home town over His claims of being the fulfillment of the prophesy in the book of Isaiah. This kind of controversy is related to the Kingdom of God. However, it is counter-productive to add trouble for doing wrong when we have enough trouble for doing what is right.

What Battles to Fight?

Through my study of the Bible and personal experience, I have come to the conclusion that there are conflicts in the spiritual and physical world. However, I have come to understand that every battle is not mine to fight. There might be battles going on all around me, but it does not mean that I am to be openly and outwardly involved in every one of them. Sometimes we need to keep our distance as well as to keep our mouths shut and pray about the situation. This is particularly true when it comes to interpersonal conflicts on the job. We have all at one time or another stuck our noses into a squabble that was none of our business and the results were disastrous. Every time we did, the cause of Christ suffered.

Satan will often try to draw us into a conflict to distract us and get our minds off of our Lord's business. Remember, we are here to do the King's business and not our own. We are on his time schedule, and we dare not squander our time or our opportunities. How many times have we gotten involved in a conflict between two parties and the two parties ended up making peace and then both declared war on us? Some people just love a good fight and do not want anyone interfering. People are funny that way. Any police officer that has had to respond to a domestic dispute can testify to that.

The point that I am trying to make is that as long as we are on the Lord's business, we cannot afford to be sidetracked by earthly matters. I am reminded of the time the Pharisees tried to trick Jesus into a controversial situation.
Matthew 22:15 Then the Pharisees went out and laid plans to trap Him in His words.
16 They sent their disciples to Him along with the Herodians. "Teacher," they said, "we know You are a man of integrity and that You teach the way of God in accordance with the truth. You aren't swayed by men, because You pay no attention to who they are.
17 Tell us then, what is Your opinion? Is it right to pay taxes to Caesar or not?"
18 But Jesus, knowing their evil intent, said, "You hypocrites, why are you trying to trap Me?
19 Show Me the coin used for paying the tax." They brought Him a denarius,
20 and He asked them, "Whose portrait is this? And whose inscription?"
21 "Caesar's," they replied. Then He said to them, "Give to Caesar what is Caesar's, and to God what is God's."

What we see in this passage is the Pharisees attempting to get Jesus in a controversial situation. If He said it was not right to pay taxes, He would be at odds with the Roman authorities. If He said it was right to pay the taxes to Rome, He would be at odds with the common people. However Jesus, operating in wisdom, replied in such a way, that the Pharisees were confounded.

Another example is when Jesus was in the region of Tyre and Sidon and a Canaanite woman pleaded with Him to heal her daughter. Jesus told her that He "was sent only to the lost sheep of Israel" (Matthew 15:21-28). As hard as it sounds, Jesus was teaching us about priorities. He was focused on the mission His Father had given to Him and He was not going to be sidetracked.

The application of this biblical story is this. There are earthly matters that are temporal and have no eternal consequences and therefore will pass away. There are spiritual matters that have eternal consequences. Most of the conflicts we see on the job have only temporal consequences. The battle for people's souls has eternal consequences. I do not mean to imply that we do not seek to make things better for those around us. Who is better qualified than the followers of the Prince of Peace to work towards peace? The Bible clearly teaches us to do good to all men (Galatians 6:10). However, we do need to seek the wisdom of God to show us when and how to do the good deeds.

We must apply godly wisdom in choosing the battles to fight because it is important to save our ammunition for the battles that count. We have all seen movies where a man was hiding from another man who was trying to shoot him. The man who was hiding would throw objects into areas away from where he was hiding and trick the other man into wasting all his ammunition. When the gunman was out of bullets, the other man would come out of hiding and subdue the gunman. This is the very same tactic that the Devil uses. He wants us to waste all our time, money, and efforts in areas away from where he is really active.

We generally only have small windows of opportunities to share the saving grace of Jesus Christ, and we cannot afford to waste them. It troubles me when I hear of a minister who is known more for his political stand than his Gospel stand. It troubles me when a pastor is known more for the saving of the environment than the saving of souls. As important as the issue of abortion is, we should not be known in our workplace as someone who is against abortion as much as we are known for Christ. Abortion is an abominable and murderous practice. However, if we spend more time talking about this subject than Christ, we have truly missed the mark. I firmly believe that we need to stand up for right, but a particular righteous cause should never overshadow our witness for Jesus. We need to be known as Christians, who because of our stand for Christ is against the ills of this world, rather than someone who is for or against a particular issue who happens to be a Christian.

Minding Our Own Business

Many of us need to mind our own business. We are not called to voice our opinion to everyone we come in contact with. The person who came up with the statement, "Everybody's got a right to my opinion," probably was not a Christian. It is amazing the number of trivial matters we get involve with. What business is it of ours if someone in another department came in late twice last week? What business is it of ours if one of our fellow employees left for lunch early yesterday as long as we were not left to do their work? Also, what business is it of ours if someone is buying a house that you believe to be out of their price range, or a truck, car, boat, watch, RV, television, etc.? What business is it of ours, if a coworker is always going to the beach, or skiing, or to a computer show, or if he takes one hour of vacation time every Friday afternoon? Mark my word saints, if we are involved in running our mouths about these things, and things like them, it will greatly diminish our effectiveness in witnessing for Christ.

Proverbs 26:17 says, " Like one who seizes a dog by the ears is a passer-by who meddles in a quarrel not his own." I have owned at least six dogs in my life time. The breeds included German Shepherds, Collies, Labrador Retrievers, mix breeds and small lap dogs. I had most of them from puppies until they were old. However, there is one thing that all of them had in common. If I pulled them by their ears they would try to bite my hand off, clear up to my elbow. Even the most cowardly of dogs will inflict harsh punishment on anyone who would be foolish or ignorant enough to pull its ears. In the same way, you risk serious consequences if you meddle in quarrels that are not our own. Even Paul wrote in First Thessalonians 4:11, "Make it your ambition to lead a quiet life, *to mind your own business* and to work with your hands, just as we told you,"

Taking Side in a Conflict

We also need to be careful about choosing sides in a conflict that does not involve us. In fact, if it does not pertain to you, the best thing we can do is to stay out of the conflict.

Those on the opposing sides in a conflict always seek to get others who are not involved on their side. This behavior is true from the schoolhouse to the courthouse to the White House. Unfortunately, it also exists in the church house. People will do anything to get others on their side. The following is their rationale. If I have more people who agree with me than those who agree with him, I feel justified in my cause, position or stand. I can be the hero, martyr and victim all at once. After all, nobody likes him; and if the Christian, the representative of God, agrees with me, that is all the better. We should not be swayed by such thinking because we are called to be peacemakers.

Let me share with you something that happened on one of my jobs. The company decided to close my section when the section head retired. Rather than lay the remaining employees off, the company decided to disperse us between other sections. The section I was sent to was known for its bickering and infighting. In this section there were two groups at war with each other. In one of these groups was an individual who seemed to be at war with anything that breathed. I even had a couple of run-ins with this person. For the sake of anonymity, I will call this person Willie. Willie was like the apostle Nathaniel, who was one of Jesus' earliest disciples. He was a man without guile or deceit (John 1:45-51). What you saw was who he was. He did not dwell in the grey areas. Black was black and white was white. You always knew where you stood with Willie. He felt that everyone was entitled to his opinion. If he did not like you, something you said, something you did, or something you wore, he would let you know. Those who like to dwell in the grey areas and like to use vague words feel threatened by the Willies of the world.

I was told by everyone that the only problem that I would have was getting along with Willie. They considered it to be impossible. As God would have it, I was transferred to his department and would have to work very closely with him. To everyone's surprise, we worked well together. He was straight forward with me, and I was straight forward with him. When the "nice" people would talk about him behind his back, I would not join in. In addition, I was careful not to receive negative comments from him about others. I believe by doing this, he trusted and respected me. I always made it a point to keep my word and to walk in integrity. He would ask me all kinds of questions about the Bible and how it related to current events and I would answer them to the best of my knowledge. At times he would try to bait me. Sometimes I would tell him that I did not know the answers. We make a big mistake when we feel that we have to have all the answers. We make an even bigger mistake when we act like we have all the answers. When we do, our hypocrisy can be seen by everyone.

Someone who was supposed to be my biggest problem ended up being my biggest blessing. Soon he was doing favors for me. Without me requesting it, he downloaded the Bible for me and put it on one of the computers at work. He brought me gifts and gave me food. He covered for me when I made mistakes. He went out of his way to show me ways to do my work better and make it easier. I was able to trust him more than anyone else in the section. If he said that he was going to do something, it was as good as done.

Though I cannot say we were the best of friends, I can say that God gave me favor with him. Proverbs 16:7 says, "When a man's ways are pleasing to the Lord, he makes even his enemies live at peace with him." I personally saw this scripture come alive in the person of Willie. I think this is significant because this was the same individual who tried to get me to file that housing discrimination claim that I talked about in the previous chapter on "Integrity" who in that chapter, I referred to as Barney.

Another reason why we need to stay out of conflict of opposing camps is that we do not know the whole story. We rarely have all the facts or the history leading up to the conflict. It is like the story of the man that asked a little boy why he was crying. The little boy replied, "Those two older boys over there have taken my plastic baseball bat that I just got for my birthday." The man went to the boys and indignantly demanded that the boys return the bat and apologize to the little boy. However, one of the boys replied, "But we had to take it because the little boy kept hitting us with it." I have rarely seen a case where either side was totally innocent. Proverbs 18:17 says, "The first to present his case seems right, until another comes forward and questions him." People have a strange habit of forgetting information that would incriminate them.

There is an interesting story in Joshua 5:13-15. The children of Israel had crossed the Jordan River and were about to attack Jericho. When Joshua was near the city, he looked up and saw a man before him with a drawn sword. He then asked the man with the sword, "Are you for us or for our enemies?" Then the man with the sword said, "Neither." and then identified himself as the commander of the Lord's army. I was baffled as to the meaning of the story. I was expecting the man with the sword to say, "You are righteous and highly favored, oh Joshua, and I am here to fight on your side to defeat your enemies." I have come to the understanding that God is on His own side. He is the potter and we are the clay. The important question is not, "Is God on my side?" It is, "Am I on God's side?" We are not blessed for the sake of ourselves. We are blessed for the sake of Christ. We are like the man with the sword. In 2 Timothy 2:3-4, we see that we are in the Lord's army, and we are not on this one's side or that one's side. Our spiritual resources are not there to add to the credibility of a foreign army's cause or to stroke someone's ego.

We Christians have fallen into the trap of being identified with deferent political parties over the years. These associations have left us wounded and feeling used. They have caused us to compromise our stands for small insignificant gains in matters that only pertain to this life. I do not believe that a single person has ever gotten saved by our alignment to earthly politics that by nature is worldly.

Complainers Beget Complainers

I want to touch on one other issue that can bring about on-the-job controversy "our associations." In Proverbs 22:24-25, it reads, "Do not make friends with a hot-tempered man, do not associate with one easily angered, or you may learn his ways and get yourself ensnared." I would like to take editorial liberty and include in this scriptural passage, someone who continuously complains. It has been my observation that those who associate with a complainer start to complain also. As the scripture passage states, "you may learn his ways and get yourself ensnared."

Complaining will often leads to conflict and conflict leads to controversy. Complaining is contagious. I have worked with employees that never had a good word to say about their job, their supervisor, or their company. They were critical of everything. They could not see anything that was right. Everything was always wrong. If the supervisor said, "Go left," they complained. If the supervisor said, "Go right," they complained. Pretty soon others were also complaining. They did not even know what they were complaining about, but that did not stop them. It does not take a whole lot to start a fire, and once it gets going good, it is very difficult to put out.

There is a phenomenon in audio engineering circles known as "feedback." This is a distorted sound that is high pitched, very loud and ear piercing. It occurs when a microphone is directed towards an audio speaker. The microphone detects the sound coming from the speaker, even if it is very small. It might be the slight hiss that comes through the speakers. The microphone creates a signal that is passed through a cable and on to an amplifier. The amplifier increases this signal and passes it through other cables to the speakers. This cycle is repeated many times in a second. What finally comes out of the speakers is the sound that went into the microphone, but the volume has been magnified by many times. What we finally hear is the ear splitting distorted noise called feedback.

Complaining and murmuring are like feedback, a loud distorted sound. It starts when an ear (microphone) detects a noise (problem). Through the nerves (cables) a signal gets passed to the hearer's brain (amplifier). The complainer's brain always amplifies what the ears have heard. It always makes it worse than it really is. The brain passes the signal through the nerves to the mouth (speaker), which makes the noise much louder than it originally was. What comes out is also distorted. Another ear picks this up and starts the cycle over and over and over again until you have an environment that is very unpleasant and uncomfortable to say the least.

God hates a complaining spirit because it causes confusion and strife, and it is always divisive. This is something that a Christian needs to avoid. If God convicts you of this sin, you need to repent and ask for His help to overcome this sin in order that you might be a better witness for Him. God is not the author of confusion (1 Corinthians 14:33), and He desires people to walk in peace and unity. The Israelites grumbled the whole time while God was bringing them into the promise land, and He judged them for it (Numbers 13:1-14:38). When the twelve spies came back to give their report, ten came back with what the scripture terms as "an evil report." I think it is more than interesting that the whole nation of Israel started grumbling based on the report of only ten men. (1

Corinthians 5:5 says, "a little bit of yeast goes through the whole loaf.") Because of the grumbling, there was no forward progress. In fact the scripture records that the ones who grumbled never proceeded beyond their circumstances.

Now we should be able to see clearly why we as Christians need to stay clear of those who constantly complain. Controversy surrounds them and if we hang around them, unnecessary controversy will surround us also. If we do not heed this advice, we will also start to complain. When we do, we become part of the problem rather than part of the solution. We become agents of confusion and strife rather than ambassadors of peace. We become peddlers of error rather than bearers of truth. We encourage hopelessness instead of faith. We promote division rather than reconciliation. We have been called to a ministry of reconciliation, not a ministry of division. God, who reconciled us to Himself through Christ, gave us the ministry of reconciliation (2 Corinthians. 5:18-19). We should be known as those who promote peace because Jesus said, "Blessed are the peacemakers, for they will be called sons of God" (Matthew 5:9).

In conclusion, we will never be able to escape controversy. It is a part of being a Christian. Jesus said, "Remember the words I spoke to you: 'No servant is greater than his master.' If they persecuted Me, they will persecute you also. If they obeyed My teaching, they will obey yours also (John 15:20)." Our convictions are diametrically opposed to the views of this world system. "In fact, everyone who wants to live a godly live in Christ will be persecuted (2 Timothy 3:12)." People will hate us because we are running against the grain. They will persecute us because we will not bow down to their idols.

1 Peter 4:15-16 says, "If you suffer, it should not be as a murderer or thief or any other kind of criminal, or even as a meddler. However, if you suffer as a Christian, do not be ashamed, but praise God that you bear that name." If we are to be in a situation of controversy, let it be because of the cause of Christ. It is very interesting that the words "even a meddler" were included

in 1 Peter 4:15-16. These verses should be a great admonition for those who do not meddle in others' affairs, as well as a stinging rebuke to those who do.

Chapter 11

God's Final Exam

A number of years have passed since I started writing this book. When I started it, I held a secular job and pastored a church. Then I gave up the secular job and worked as a full-time pastor. After that period, I worked two other secular jobs before returning to work full-time pastoring at another church. I am now working on a secular job and I am not currently pastoring. Because of my experiences as a Christian on secular jobs and a pastor, I have had the opportunity to test the principles that I have written about in this book.

The last secular job that I had before my last pastoring position would be "trial by fire." I had to go beyond the theory and theology and apply all the advice I have given you. This job provided the most difficult circumstances that I have ever faced. The Lord was about to give me the final exam. This exam would be comprehensive. It would go well beyond the things I had experienced before. It would test my integrity, character, faith, and my motives. The tests that the Lord gives are more than simply sessions to show Him how much scripture we can recite. He gives them to reveal to us whether we can apply the scriptures we know, that is, can we obey what His word tells us to do. This testing is important because God uses it as an instrument to help transform us into the image of Christ.

A Disastrous Beginning

My last secular job started with great expectations. The interview process had gone well and my supervisors told me that they were expecting me to bring about much needed changes in the department. I was also confident that I would be instrumental in bringing about these changes. I had the experience, motivation, education, and the people skills that would be needed to get the job done. I had already been where the management wanted to go.

Though it was not a perfect technical match with what I had previously been doing, I saw no problems in making the transition. I saw it as another opportunity to broaden my experience base. I was even getting an increase in salary that I really needed. The Lord had prepared a place for me again, but His thoughts were far from my thoughts. That bright sunshiny day was about to turn into a total solar eclipse.

My first six months were an utter disaster. Things were going very badly. What ever could go wrong did. In spite of my best efforts, I was making huge mistakes in the technical test I was required to perform. The mistakes were coming in bunches, and they were the kind of mistakes that did not show themselves for about a week after they were made. If they had shown up as I was performing the test, I could have made corrections as I went along. Unfortunately, by the time the test results came back, there was no way to repair the damage. To further complicate matters, it was difficult for me to remember what I could have done the week earlier to cause the errors. The test was known to be a difficult one to perform, however, compared to most of what I had done in my career, it was not particularly technically difficult. I kept saying to myself, "This is not that hard! What is the problem?"

I would come in early, work through lunch, and stay late. One time I was called into the manager's office because I was there so late and so many times that it made him look like he was not giving me the help I needed. Many times I was the last to leave. There were times when I would leave so late that the buses had stopped running. Once I had to walk five miles to get home. I ended up getting home after midnight because I had missed the last bus, and I still had to be back early the next morning. I kept telling myself that things had to get better. I was better than what I was producing, and things did get better for about a week. It was just enough time to build my hopes up before they came crashing down all around me like a fallen crystal chandelier.

I was on an emotional roller coaster ride. When things went bad, I did not know why, and when things went good, I did not know why. What I did know was that I was coming to the end of my probation period, and things did not look good. I was accustomed to going into jobs and turning situations around. I had prided myself in this area, but for the first time in my career, I was part of the problem and not the solution. Adding to my problems, there was at least one supervisor who desired to fire me. He told this to at least one employee who worked under me. That employee passed it on to me. This information caused my stress level to significantly increase! But the Lord was at work in this situation. I will reveal how later.

It is amazing when you are having problems and things are not going well how the devil can stir up others to come against you. I was now being accused of many things that were not my fault and that I was not responsible for. However, it seemed that everything that went wrong was being laid at my feet. There were things done and said to me that were just not right. This situation reminds me of how the Bible portrays Satan as standing before God and accusing the saints (Rev. 12:10). The problem is that a lot of what he says is true. We all have sinned and fallen short of the glory of God. We all have missed the mark.

Adding to the criticism of my work were personal attacks. There was talk questioning my intelligence. I started hearing rumors about me being mentally slow. Others took the position that I did not care about my work. I kept crying out to the Lord and telling myself that I have to do better. I kept reminding myself that I represent the King of the universe, I am a reflection of God, I am an ambassador for Christ.

I was called into the section supervisor's office and reprimanded, to the glee of some. How could I effectively witness for Christ to my managers and supervisors if all they could see was someone whose work was a constant source of irritation? The end of my probation period was not far off, and I was not confident that I would be retained. At this job, once you made it through the probation period, it was very difficult for you to be fired. However during the probation period, you could be released with no questions asked. Management did not have to justify their decisions. I was approached again about another analysis that had gone badly. After the supervisor left me, I had no peace, and my joy was gone. I was utterly bewildered regarding the circumstance of my career. I fasted. I prayed. My wife prayed. Others prayed for me. No matter what I did, my situation was not changing. There was no improvement.

Then the Spirit of God spoke to my spirit and said, "Why does the canary cease to sing? If your situation never changes, will you be miserable for the rest of your life?" My spirit cried back with a resounding, "NO!" There is a joy in God that goes far beyond our circumstances, and I was created in Christ Jesus to live in that joy. I determined at that time to hide myself in the "Cleft of the Rock" and wait for the storm to blow over. It did not happen all at once, but the peace of God started to abide and the joy started to return. I learned that God is a shelter in the time of storm. You will never truly know that until you are in a storm. You cannot get that type of knowledge from a theology book. You can know something about it, but there is a knowing that only comes through personally experiencing it in the midst of a trial. I still did the best I could and constantly looked for ways to improve. I did not throw my hands up in the air and sing "Que sera, sera." I was now refocused on the "Shepherd of my soul."

I would like to say that focusing on Jesus ended the storm, but I cannot because the worst was yet to come. The darkest times were yet looming. With the peace came extra persecution. Non-believers are always confused by the works of God in a believer's life. They tend to come to the wrong conclusions. The peace of God in my life showed on my countenance, but was mistaken for apathy. Of course, the opposite was true for reasons they could not know. I got comments from supervisors that I acted like I did not care. Considering the amount of time and effort that I continued to put into my work, which had not diminished during this period, the comments were contradictory. One of them, who was actually sympathetic to my situation said to me, "Come on, Tom. Shedding a tear would help." What they did not understand at the time was that just because everything around you is falling apart, you do not have to fall apart. Literally, every one of the supervisors was on blood pressure medicine, and I felt no inclination to join their ranks.

I understood that the management had a responsibility for the quality of work that was produced. If the work that was produced by those they were managing was poor, it was a reflection on their work performance. I knew that they were being called into question by those to whom they had to answer. They were under a lot of pressure also. I was conscience of the fact that others were affected by what was happening. Our lives are intertwined with others. No one lives to themselves or dies to themselves. We cannot be so consumed by our own troubles to the point where we become oblivious to the sufferings of those around us. Even in the midst of Jesus' passion, He had compassion for the plight of others. He healed the High Priest servant's ear (John 18:10-11) that Peter had cut off. He ministered to the thief on the cross (Luke 23:32-43). He assigned John to take care of His mother (John 19:25-27). He even prayed for those who sent Him to the cross (Luke 23:24).

During this period I never stopped praying for my manger and supervisors. I did not pray so much for them to treat me better. I prayed for them to be able to hear God's voice and discover His plans for their lives. I prayed for the various problems that I knew they were facing on and off the job. I prayed for them in personal areas that bound them. I prayed for their salvation. I prayed for their marriages, spouses, relationships with their children, financial needs, legal problems, and health problems. Everyday before I came into work, I would pray for them by name as well as for everyone else I worked with. Of course there were also times during the workday that I would bring their names before the throne of God.

Vindicated by God

When I came to my probation review, I knew I was in a very vulnerable position, but I went in trusting God and with peace in my heart. My life was in His hands, and so I was confident that whatever happened, He would cause all things to work for my good. In deed, He was working behind the scenes. My manager had made some major gaffs in regard to my training. He had not adhered to some proper procedures.

As mentioned before, my immediate supervisor, for the purposes of anonymity I will call him Ralph, had told at least one person who was at a lower grade than me that he wanted to fire me. To make matters worse the department had been plagued for years by lawsuits and potential lawsuits of alleged discrimination and misconduct. I had enough evidence on them to take them down with me or at least cause them some major grief.

During my time at the meeting, I shared some things that I felt were unfair and improper in regard to the way my situation was handled as well as owning up to my failures. Before I went into the meeting, I decided that I was going to let the Lord fight my battles for me. It is important for every Christian to understand that if we choose to fight for ourselves, God will stay out of it and let us handle the whole thing. The battle either belongs to us or it belongs to the Lord. We are the ones who must choose.

By the time the meeting was over, my probation had been extended and I felt that I was treated relatively fair. Ralph was reprimanded, and I was given the added assignment of reporting back to his boss in regard to Ralph's progress. I felt like I was living the book of Esther. The Bible says, "Do not touch My anointed ones; do My prophets no harm" (1 Chronicles 16:22). It also say, "No weapon forged against you will prevail, and you will refute every tongue that accuses you. This is the heritage of the servants of the LORD, and this is their vindication from Me, declares the Lord" (Isaiah 54:17).

There was no joy in me at Ralph's reprimand. When you earnestly pray for someone on a daily basis, you cannot be pleased when God's judgment comes into their life. I recognized that he was new at being a supervisor and that he lacked people skills. Boy, did he lack people skills! If you earnestly pray for God's heart, He will grant you His heart for others. God's desire is to bless and prosper people and that is what I wanted for Ralph. I took the opportunity to report to his supervisor when I saw improvement and if I noticed things he was doing right. Why is it that we are silent when someone does something right, but very vocal when they do something wrong? When others were critical of him, I refused to chime in and as I had opportunity, I would say something positive. By doing this, others turned against me, even though I did the same for them. As I stated in a previous chapter, if someone dislikes a certain person, they want everyone to dislike that person. Jesus said in Matthew 5:46, "If you love those who love you, what reward will you get?"

Christmas was approaching and I wanted to give Ralph a gift. "Bless those who curse you, pray for those who mistreat you" (Luke 6:28). I had three immediate supervisors, including him, and I bought each a bottle of sparkling cider and left them on their desks. Ralph was not in that day, but when he saw me, with a bewildered look on his face, said, "Thank you, Tom, that was very kind of you." For the first time I sensed a change in his spirit. His supervisor would eventually tell me that Ralph had confessed that he was wrong about me. Many people might think something, but there is a difference between thinking something and speaking it.

Suffering for God's Glory

The following year, I unexpectedly had to go through heart surgery. Lightning struck my home and set it on fire, and I literally had to rescue my youngest son from the burning room. My family and I lived in two different apartments and had to fight with contractors for the next five and a half months. To top my list of woes, we were involved in an accident with a deer late one night.

But in spite of all my personal troubles, I saw God turn my adversaries into my greatest allies. During this time, my life was on full display to those I worked with. Everything I said and did was examined. My life was a living epistle, fully read by men. It was during this time that I learned that every hard time you go through is not about you. Sometimes our suffering is for the benefit of others. Jesus' experience supports this statement. His suffering was not because of anything He had done. It was for the purpose of many coming to know God and to save them from peril. Job suffered, not because of sin or a lack of faith. He suffered for the glory of God. How many times have we told God to use us as He wills, and then thought He was unfair when He did things we did not envision or understand? What we really mean is, "Lord, use me in the way that I want to be used."

I believe that it was my witness in the midst of adversity and suffering that turned their hearts. The Lord answered my question, "How could I be an effective witness for Him if all that my manager and supervisors could see was my poor work performance?" The answer was "through suffering." I am not implying that this is true in every situation, but there are cases where it is absolutely necessary.

Suffering is not a popular subject in the Church. There is an epidemic of preaching on how you can get all your desires met, how I can be blessed, how I can get rich, how I can succeed, how I can have divine health, how I can get that house, car, promotion, raise, live in that special neighborhood, get that husband or wife. We want to know how we can remove all pain and discomfort from our lives. How many conferences do you know about that have had the title "Suffering for the Kingdom." Jesus told Anninas, "I will show him (Paul) how much he must suffer for My name" (Acts 9:16). Paul wrote, "I want to know Christ and the power of His resurrection and the fellowship of sharing in His sufferings, becoming like Him in His death," (Phil 3:10). What are you willing to suffer to see others come into the kingdom of God? I am convinced that it is not when everything is going well that we have our greatest witness. It is during our times of trials and adversities.

God Gave Me Favor

It was during and after this time that God gave me great favor with my manager and supervisors. There was an open door into their hearts that only months earlier had been closed. My advice was being sought after. In fact, my advice was sought on many topics, including marriage, child rearing, finances, careers, employee and personal relationships. I was even getting questions about the Church that led to questions about the Lord. I was invited to go out to eat with them. God even used me as an unofficial advisor to the manager. One time after praying on my lunch hour (Yes, the Lord had blessed me to the point that I did not have to work through my lunch); God revealed to me a solution to a problem the manager was having with some employees. I shared with him what the Lord said. Some of what I told him could have been taken as a mild rebuke of his management, but the Lord had truly given me great liberty and favor.

The Lord also started blessing me in my work. In fact, it seemed like everything I laid my hands on prospered. As I have previously stated, I was being sought after for advice. I would hear, "What does Tom think about this or that?" I was asked by my supervisors to speak to the department on certain technical procedures. Upper management would stop me in the hallway and discuss technical matters as well as other issues. I was even selected to be part of a hiring interview team. "I will repay you for the years the locusts have eaten. . . ." (Joel 2:25).

At my last job performance appraisal my manager told me that he could not pay me for what I was worth to the department. He was not just referring to my actual work. He recognized that there were many intangibles that could not be put down on paper. I think he viewed me like Potiphar viewed Joseph (Genesis 39:1-6).

It can be a wonderful thing when people start to realize that God is with you. They do not want any thing to happen to you because they see they are being blessed because of you. One time, while attempting to improve a certain procedure, I made a major mistake that released some toxic fumes into the lab. One of the persons who worked in the lab feigned sick behind the fumes. This person was always claiming some ailment. This claim set the stage for major troubles for me as well as the department. This time Ralph did everything he could to shield me from the repercussion of my blunder. It was his job to write me up over this, but as I sat with him it was obvious that he was struggling over the process. In fact he put me in the most positive light that he could. There were also other times when he defended me in front of other employees. I saw God turn an adversary into my greatest ally.

Parting with Victory

After working there for about two years, I was asked to accept an Associate Pastor position at the church I was attending. I am grateful that the Lord blessed me in that this new position did not open up before the storm was over. By His grace, He allowed me to leave as an employee respected for my character and my work. The Church has come up with a lot of "bail out" theology, but God has called us to be more than conquers. This means He wants us to be victorious over our circumstances in life. Not only does He want us to face our giants, He wants us to conquer them. He wants us to overcome our fears as well as our failures. He wants to transform us from being a victim to being a victor. If the new position had come up when the times were hard, I would have wondered for the rest my life if it was from the Lord or was it just something I accepted because I wanted to get out of my life's circumstances. If the Lord had bailed me out, I would have missed seeing the salvation of the Lord working through me for the changing of men's hearts. It is also doubtful that I would have written this chapter of the book. "This is the Lord's doing, and it is marvelous in our eyes" (Matthew 21:42).

I believe that it was God's will for me to accept the Associate Pastors' position, but I believe just as strongly that the position I was about to leave was just as much His calling on my life for that time. I had to walk in just as much of God's anointing on that job as I would have on staff at my church. It might be argued that I needed a greater anointing to be successful on a secular job.

God Gives the Assignments

I cannot emphasize enough to the readers of this book that though we are not all pastors who work at a church, we are still called to be missionaries and evangelists in the areas God has placed us in. We are His ambassadors to this lost and dying world. We are His lights that shine in the darkness. If we are truly walking with the Lord, we do not choose our assignments. We accept His calling. When the Lord asks who will go for Him, we should say what Isaiah said, "Here I am; send me" (Isaiah 6:8).

To my brothers and sisters who gain your salaries from the Church, I ask the following questions. Would you consider it a step down if God wanted you to work in a secular environment? Would you think that God has forsaken you? Would you think He was unfair? Do you think you are too good or too spiritual to work outside your church? Would the Lord have to drag you out while you are kicking and screaming? What if He wanted to send you to work in a factory, a school, the entertainment industry, or in politics? Could it be that *your* attitudes towards secular jobs are the biggest hindrance to the individuals in your congregation fulfilling their calling in their careers? Maybe the biggest difference between those who work at a church and those who do not is the source of their income. Selah

Retrospection

As I look back on that period of my life, I view it with great awe and even fondness. The test was over and though I would not want to go through it again I would not trade it for anything. Time and print does not allow me to give you every detail of the story and if anyone who was a part of this story reads this book and thinks I have left something out, you are probably right. Much of what was not included in this book has to do with my sensitivity towards people's feelings. There were also many matters that needed to be kept private. The Bible says in First Corinthians 13 that love covers. Love does not seek to embarrass and expose others. There were many things shared in confidence by unbeliever with me. If I see them twenty years from now, I want them to feel that their confidence in me was well founded. Christians should be known as a people to whom others could safely trust to share the deepest parts of their soul.

God did some amazing things during that time, and the fruit of my labors continues to grow. I was invited to return to the company of my test for a Christmas party two years later. Most of the same people were still there. I was warmly greeted and some told me how I had touched their lives. Ralph was also there. Right before I left the company he told me how much he had learned from me. At that gathering, he informed me that he was attending a Bible-believing church, and he was even attending the Wednesday evening Bible study. I told him that I believed that I was specifically sent to that company for him. God had specifically fashioned me to be that perfect tool for Him to do a work in Ralph's life. With a look of wonder on his face, he said he believed that this was true. It never ceases to amaze me how much God will invest just to reach one lost sinner.

Does God so love the people at your job that He would send you, His beloved son or daughter, that whoever believes in the "Him" that is inside of you would not perish, but have everlasting life? Selah.

NOTES